Shayna Hubers, Killer

Pete Dove

Published by Trellis Publishing, 2021.

While every precaution has been taken in the preparation of this book, the publisher assumes no responsibility for errors or omissions, or for damages resulting from the use of the information contained herein.

SHAYNA HUBERS, KILLER

First edition. July 15, 2021.

Copyright © 2021 Pete Dove.

ISBN: 979-8224194605

Written by Pete Dove.

SHAYNA HUBERS, KILLER
PETE DOVE

The Impenetrable Problem of Potential Domestic Abuse

A Kentucky prison is home to a woman of immense potential; now her life stands in tatters. A promising legal career is curtailed as a result of an act of unimaginable violence. There are no witnesses to that violence. One element of it is accepted by both prosecution and defense. The other is not. This aspect may, or may not, even exist. Truth becomes impossible to determine. A jury, uninformed and unqualified, are forced to reach a decision, the outcome of which will determine people's futures. Evidence is scarce; the decision they reach is one that can never be guaranteed as just, however honestly it is made.

Shayna Hubers was born in Lexington, the second largest of Kentucky's cities. One which is home to a population of around a third of a million people. It is a wealthy city in a wealthy county and boasts a wide range of cultural and historical structures. That one in four of its population hold a degree, and more than ten per cent of the people of Lexington hold a master's qualification is evidence that this is an affluent, thriving center. Certainly, whatever, if any, problems Shayna collected during her early life, they were not related to deprivation. Not that she has ever claimed that they were.

Shayna grew to become a tall, slim brunette, five feet eight and a half inches tall and weighing in at a healthy one hundred and twenty pounds. Her long, wavy hair and striking blue eyes embellish a face which is often broken by her wide smile. That engaging grin breaks out, even today, as she enters her ninth year behind bars. On the horizon her thirtieth birthday beckons. A woman who should be entering the prime of her life instead remains incarcerated behind bars. Meanwhile, her potential drips away, the victim of a judicial system which, in her case, many argue is not fit for purpose. Maybe. It is impossible to know for sure.

Ryan Poston may well have been headed for great things too. He was a bright man, and a well-travelled one. He'd attended school not only in the US, (at the Blessed Sacrament School in Fort Mitchell,

Kentucky) but also at the International School in Manila, Philippines and the International School of Geneva, in Switzerland. The latter two are fee paying private schools, the first a strongly religious institution, itself an elite institution.

Poston took up a university spot in Indiana, majoring in three subjects – history, political science and law. He completed his academic career by taking a degree at the prestigious Salmon P Chase College of Law which is based in Northern Kentucky.

Shayna was, like her boyfriend to be, an academically successful child. Unlike Ryan, however, she was little more than a minor when the two got together. Aged just nineteen, she was nine years her boyfriend's junior when the two discovered each other via Facebook, that well-known source of stable relationships. Although, in fact, there was already a very tenuous connection between the couple. Ryan's step cousin was Carissa Carlisle, and she was a friend of Shayna. Ryan and Shayna first got to know each other in 2011, and their relationship quickly flourished into a romantic one. As stated, Shayna was a successful academic, and was studying at the University of Kentucky in Lexington at this time. Her subject was psychology, and after graduating cum laude (that is, in the top quarter of her class) she remained in the academic world, studying for a master's degree in counselling for schools.

Sarah Robinson grew up in Lexington with Shayna and recalls her academic prowess. 'I thought she was, close to genius, in my opinion,' she said. 'I mean, she was always in AP classes, always getting A's in everything.'

But if the two on and off lovers shared a strong educational pedigree it was also one which was highly volatile. Hubers said: 'I gave him the nose job he wanted,' after she had shot Ryan. Six times. While they were together in his luxury apartment.

Such a comment as that made by Shayna is damning. Surely, it means the twenty-year minimum sentence she is currently serving is more than deserved? If only matters were that simple. In this case, they most definitely are not.

Prior to the shooting, Shayna claimed that Ryan threw her across the room and into a bookshelf. However, the police's argument is that, since they maintain they found no evidence of any such assault, it did not occur. A photo they took of the bookshelf shows a collection of ten bullets, each of a different size, which are lined up on the top of the shelf, near a gun and next to a decorative tobacco pipe. The police state that had Shayna been thrown into the bookshelf; the bullets would have been disturbed from their tidy row.

They seem to have discounted, or not considered, that this aspect of the altercation could have occurred in the early stages of the incident, and the bullets replaced by either Ryan or Shayna. This oversight is symptomatic of Shayna and Ryan's entire case. The picture presented by all elements of the arguments against her is ones of extremes, a caricature almost. As though one or other – perhaps both – of the partners were acting in extreme, unmitigated, violence, like some character from a slasher flick or horror movie. Whereas, in reality, the violence in domestic incidents often rises and falls, fluctuating by the second. It is certainly conceivable that the bullets were disturbed, then replaced in a calm moment, before the situation escalated once more.

Further, other evidence points to the fact that Shayna was involved in some kind of struggle. Police took photographs in the immediate aftermath of her arrest – she was taken to the station shortly after her 911 call. These pictures show bruising on her arm. It is not especially heavy, but equally, was taken perhaps before it had developed as much as it might. The bruising is circular, and consistent with her wrist being gripped tightly. The authorities, however, dismissed the photos as being out of line with Shayna's claims of a violent struggle.

Yet even in this moment, the evidence presented is shaky once more. Shayna is known to have been acting extremely strangely in the police cell on the night of her arrest, which occurred immediately after she reported the shooting. Footage shows her dancing around, singing 'Amazing Grace', paper coffee cups demonstrating the recent gathering that had been in the interrogation room. In such a volatile emotional state, it is highly likely that she may have deliberately or unconsciously exaggerated the extent of the fracas with Ryan. Once more, it appears from the outside as though a lack of proper awareness of the impact of domestic violence was applied in this case.

Shayna's mother is a retired teacher and remains convinced of her daughter's innocence. Whilst it is not in doubt that Shayna fired the shots which killed Ryan Poston, and discharged no less than six bullets into him, she remains convinced that only a severe, life threatening, episode would prompt her daughter to act in such an out of character manner. To Sharon, Shayna is a talented academic who is fundamentally a peaceful person.

A key piece of evidence occurred during police questioning. 'He's very vain,' said Hubers. 'One of our last conversations we had that was good was that he wants to get a nose job, and I shot him right here. I gave him his nose job he wanted. I broke it.'

The reaction to this comment from the police team conducting the interviews is telling. 'My jaw dropped,' said Highland Heights Police Chief Bill Birkenhauer, on hearing her comments. 'I was like, "Did she really just say that?"'

No consideration from the officer that her claims that Poston was abusive towards her might carry some truth, resulting in her anger. Just astonishment at her words. Was this senior law enforcer, or any of the others involved in her interrogation, trained in dealing with victims of domestic violence? (If, indeed, Shayna was one such victim – a fact unproven). The Chief's reaction seems to suggest either not, or that any training he had undertaken had made little impact upon him.

Other footage, taken when she was alone, was also used to support the police's case. This footage included her singing and dancing in the interview room. Equally, her questions about life behind bars seemed to have been interpreted, in some quarters at least, as signs of her guilt. However, a young woman who has no experience at all of prison life might well ask such elementary questions as to her ability to shower in private, and whether she could keep her phone.

Nevertheless, at her trial a psychologist did report that Shayna suffered from psychological disorders. Dr Thomas Schact called her a narcissist. The way she spoke out loud to herself during breaks from her interviews with the police also suggests either a woman attempting to create a story about herself for future reference, or one who does (or did) suffer from mental health illnesses. 'I don't know if anyone will ever want to marry me if they know that I killed a boyfriend in self-defense; not funny,' she was recorded saying to herself. Along with 'I have two papers due Monday that I haven't…doesn't matter now.'

However, the police also reported catching her, during her dances around her interview room, calling 'I killed him, I killed him.'

'This was one of the strangest things, when she was doing that dancing, snapping her fingers and twirling around almost as if she was proud of it,' said Detective Birkenhauer later. A genuine assessment of a woman who has committed a serious crime? Or a reinforcement of his own self-fulfilling prophesy regarding her guilt?

Cecily Miller shared a cell with Shayna at the Campbell County Detention center; she testified that Shayna seemed 'carefree' about the shooting she admits to carrying out, albeit for differing reasons to those for which she was convicted. So, this is a not cut and dried case. It is just that it seems to have been presented as one by the prosecution team, the police, and the media. As though justice was about winning or losing, rather than finding the truth.

But there are two sides to the story. It is only natural that Ryan's family take the part of their son. After the original sentence was handed down, Jay, Ryan's father, issued a statement. 'It has been three long and brutal years as we sought justice for Ryan,' he said. 'Today, we embrace that justice, and yet we do not feel joy on this day.' He ended the statement by re-affirming the grief suffered by the family. 'We now move forward with our lives,' he wrote, 'with our memories and our grief.'

Ryan's stepfather, too, was proud of his stepson. 'I was hard on him at times because I have high expectations,' he admitted. Peter Carter also recalled the emotional uncertainty he felt at dating another woman whilst still ostensibly going out with Shayna. 'He was not happy with what was going on,' Carter stated.

Matt Herren was not a relative of Ryan's, but he was a close friend, and he was bemused by the killing. 'I think about him every day,' he said. 'You don't think something like that is every going to happen to someone you know.'

He continued: 'He's the type of person that you want in your life. Not just a friend, but a loving son, a protective, adoring older brother. He had three younger sisters that he absolutely adored.'

Shayna's case first came to court in April of 2015 and lasted for two weeks. Later in the year, prior to sentencing, Judge Fred A Stine stated, 'It's probably as cold blooded an act as I've been associated with in the criminal justice system.' He went on to sentence her to forty years in prison, with a requirement that she serve at least eighty-five per cent of the tariff. (Later, that sentence would be reduced). 'It's clear Ryan Poston had some demons that he was fighting, I don't think you've recognized that you have any yet,' the judge continued. Were these 'demons' references to a violent nature? The judge would not elucidate on his observation.

Laura Kirkwood was a juror at Shayna's first trial. The accused's defense of self-defense in the face of an abusive relationship was one with which she held no sympathy. 'At no point did I buy the battered girlfriend defense,' she said after the trial. 'She took the key for the house to get back in. She was free to leave and did not. I did not see any evidence of physical abuse.' However, she defended the jury's decision not to recommend a full life sentence. 'A life sentence was too long that possibly, maybe if she is rehabilitated, she could do some good when she gets out. She will be a different person when she gets out,' the former juror said.

During her trials, the prosecution claimed that Shayna killed Ryan in a fit of anger after he attempted to break up with her. At the time, he was also dating Audrey Bolte, a former Miss Ohio who held that crown at the time back in 2012. However, Shayna's defense was, and still remains, that she shot the boyfriend in self-defense. Her 999 call after the shooting was played in court and seemed to back up her claims. During the call, and in subsequent police interviews, Shayna maintained that Ryan was frequently violent and had in fact been assaulting her when she grabbed his gun and shot him. Six times.

But the line taken by Laura Kirkwood displays a gross ignorance of domestic violence matters – not that there is any particular reason why she should be an expert in the field. It is well established that women (and men) who become involved in such relationships frequently find it extremely difficult to extricate themselves from them. Their abusive partners are not usually cartoon bad guys (or women, for that matter) whose demeanors immediately mark them out as people to avoid. Their own abusive behavior is frequently a consequence of their own mental health issues, and often such perpetrators are highly skilled at disguising their behavior and at inflicting harm that is not always visible.

Of course, there is only Shayna's word that this abuse did take place, and such a line might have been a clever, if unoriginal, tactic from her own desire to avoid facing the consequences of her actions. If so, it was a strategy supported by her defense counsel. However, we do not know the extent of the problems in her relationship with Ryan – just that they were considerable. To make the assumption that simply because Shayna did not walk away from her partner is proof that she was not abused is, to be honest, uninformed. It is a standpoint not backed by either proper psychological evidence or research.

Shayna was, for example, not given a key to either the luxurious Highland Heights condo in which Ryan and, often, she lived, nor to its pool house. The judge used this as evidence that she was not co-habitating with her boyfriend, although Shayna maintained the opposite, insisting that she cleaned, cooked, decorated for the couple, and used the condo as her own home. Again, if such a situation were true, or even partly true, to deny her the right to a key, or to use the pool facility, is very strange, even if legal. It could be considered as evidence of a controlling attitude from Ryan in their relationship. Such an outlook is often found in those guilty of domestic abuse.

There is more. Shayna claimed that Ryan was threatening her with his gun when she grabbed it from his hands and shot him. 'He was right in front of me and he reached down and grabbed the gun,' she told the emergency services during her 911 call. 'I grabbed it out of his hands and pulled the trigger.'

Again, Laura Kirkwood's response to this action, if shared by the full jury, is evidence of a group of people failing to understand the true nature of domestic violence. 'I did think that after at least the first bullet – when she didn't call for help, didn't call 911, kept shooting him – that definitely it was murder,' said the former juror.

Of course, Shayna was found guilty at her second trial as well. However, the grounds for dismissal of the first ruling, to which we will turn shortly, and the fact that she had been publicly castigated after that, means that any subsequent trial faces the accusation of being unfair. That the jury would already have made up its mind.

Kirkwood's statement displays a failure to understand the panic, the fear, the anger of being threatened with a gun by a person who is, potentially, already prone to violence. There are very few people who, faced with such a life-threatening situation, will be able to remove the gun, shoot once to disable their attacker, and then calmly seek help. Especially when the attacker is a person with whom a close tie is held. And especially when the threatened person is a woman, and physically much weaker than her attacker. And finally, especially when the victim has already been identified as one who suffers from emotional trauma.

However, not all the evidence points towards a miscarriage of justice, morally even if not legally, in this case. We have already seen Shayna's ill-judged comment about giving Ryan the 'nose job' he had professed to want. She also made the following statement to police: 'I knew he was going to die a very slow and painful death. He was twitching and moaning, but I knew he was already dead.'

The angle Shayna presents is one disputed by some of Ryan's own close friends and family. Tom Awadalla was one such close mate. He said 'He (Ryan) just wasn't able to (end their relationship). He was too nice, didn't want to hurt her feelings. Another friend, Brian Stewart, took a similar stance.

'He did feel duty bound to let her down easy,' he said. Sometimes, as well, texts and social media messages Shayna sent to her friends would return to haunt her. 'When I go to the shooting range with Ryan tonight,' she posted to her friend Christie Oyler, 'I want to turn around and shoot and kill him and play like it's an accident.' However, the friend did not take the missive seriously, as indeed, it may not have been meant.

Ryan Poston was a keen gun user. His ex-girlfriend, who predated Shayna, explained as much. 'He always had them (weapons),' she reported. 'He would have one in his boot. He would have them in his holster.' Poston also kept an artillery vest in his cupboard, which vied for space with his neckties.

Another message Shayna posted indicated the turmoil she felt at some of the cruel things she believed Ryan had said to her. 'He says he is only with me because I make him feel so awful when I cry. My love has turned to hate.'

It was only a year before the judge was required to reconsider his comments about the 'cold blooded' killer. The state law of Kentucky prohibits convicted felons from serving on a jury. In Shayna's case, though, the net designed to prevent such a scenario proved to be filled with very large holes. Judge Stine was required to overturn the conviction and grant a new trial. The juror was unnamed, but had apparently pleaded guilty (something he 'doesn't remember') to falling behind on child support payments more than two decades prior to Shayna's trial, and said that he did not realize that he counted as a convicted felon.

The matter emerged as Shayna's legal team attempted to prepare her appeal. One of her lawyers recognized the name of the juror in question, realizing that she had represented him at his own child support proceedings trial in the early 1990s. However, the reaction of the media at the time indicated that, in some quarters at least, Shayna's guilt was already proven.

'This has got to be maddening for not just the prosecutor but for the judge who has to now overturn a verdict based on an inadvertent mistake,' said Dan Abrams, who was a legal analyst for ABC news at the time. No mention, then, for the years of torment and the stress and agony of the trial through which Shayna had suffered. Deserved, of course, if she was guilty, but decidedly not if she were innocent and acting only in self-defense, as she has claimed all along.

The analyst went on to develop his theory, suggesting that the failure of the state to organize its jury system properly was somehow in the defense team's interests. 'Since there was a conviction in the first case, the defense can now review their strategy and try to fine tune it,' he continued, 'possibly make some changes. But in the end, there is still a lot of evidence against her.'

More reasonably, Poston's own family were understandably disappointed with the news, but were at least steadfast in their beliefs. 'If we must endure another trial, we do so with absolute confidence that justice shall again be served,' they said in a statement.

Love did reach out to Shayna as she sat incarcerated in her prison cell following the inevitable second conviction. Sadly, it did not last long. Unique Taylor is a transgender woman, and the two married in a two-minute-long jailhouse wedding in June 2018. Whether or not the relationship could ever have survived is, of course, just speculation. However, the support of the prison service did little to further the relationship. Even the ceremony itself was grudgingly granted.

'There is a Supreme Court decision that mandates that it is a fundamental right and if they want to get married while they are in prison we have to allow it,' said Campbell County Jailer James A Daley in a curmudgeonly manner. However, although the law required that the ceremony be allowed to go ahead, the Campbell County authorities did everything in their powers to ensure it was as unrewarding as possible. Not only did the ceremony last only two minutes, Shayna and Unique were not even allowed in the same room. 'We had them in two separate little cells where they could hear each other and that was about it,' continued Daley. The couple were denied physical contact in jail following their wedding. Under such circumstances, it is no surprise that the marriage did not last, Shayna's attorney stating the impossibility of maintaining, let alone developing, any kind of relationship under such circumstances.

Whilst continuing to maintain her innocence of murder, and appearing as a double victim – firstly of domestic abuse and secondly of a judicial system which remains, it seems, unable to understand the true impact of domestic violence, Shayna Hubers was recently dealt another blow in her search for justice as she defines it. Her attempts to appeal her conviction were dismissed by the Kentucky Supreme Court in September of 2020. On this occasion Shayna's team had argued that problems existed with jury selection and also the location of her trial. But the Supreme Court dismissed their plea.

The case of Shayna Hubers and Ryan Poston is an outstandingly difficult one. Only one person can know the real truth of what happened that June day in 2012. That is Shayna Hubers. She is very clear. Her relationship with Ryan was very much on and off. It was a relationship both wished to end, but neither could bring themselves to make the break.

Ryan was cheating on his girlfriend by dating another woman. He claimed to feel bad about doing this, but it did not stop his actions. The relationship was strange in any case; Ryan refused to allow his girlfriend a key to the condo she effectively shared with him, although she had access to a spare when she wanted it.

Something occurred during that evening, and Shayna seized a gun and shot her boyfriend six times, killing him. According to Shayna what happened was that, not for the first time, Ryan attacked her, assaulted her, and threatened to kill her while waving a gun in front of her face, and gripping her arm.

Shayna wrestled the weapon from him and shot him dead. In the process, she discharged six bullets into him. Fifteen minutes or so later, she called 911 and reported what she had done, claiming self defense as the reason for her actions.

If all of this is true, surely not one civilized nation on earth could fail to hold sympathy with her actions. Everybody has the right to defend themselves in a life or death situation, and nobody can predict how an untrained person will react to such a scenario. Firing multiple shots in a state of anger, fear, horror, and emotional lack of control is not an unbelievable way to have acted.

The police and prosecutors seem to see this event differently. Shayna, to them, is a disturbed young woman distraught that her boyfriend is about to end their relationship, and in a fit of teenaged pique, she shoots him dead.

What they, the prosecutors and the jury (if the one member of Shayna's original trial who spoke out is typical) seem to have ignored is that domestic abuse is insidious, shattering and confidence destroying. Victims find their ability to react normally severely impaired. The law allows for an intruder into a home to be challenged with deadly physical force, if circumstances dictate, but (it seems) not if that attacker is a partner.

But on the other side, there is no definite evidence in this case that Shayna was the victim of such abuse, either on the night she killed her boyfriend, or in the time leading up to this.

What we are arguing here is that, maybe, more consideration should have been given to the idea that such a scenario was indeed playing out.

Because justice is not about winning or losing; it is about finding the truth and acting upon that fact. Fairly.

A SERIAL KILLER'S ROAD TRIP

Nathan Nixon

Charles Starkweather

The 1950's for the United States of America is best remembered as some of the most trying times in the history of the nation. While the early 1950's saw the baby boom, the late half of the decade was marred by civil instability and mistrust. Many Americans, especially those in the southern United States, lost their trust in the American dream as well as the government. Many of those Americans took their destiny into their own hands.

Charles Starkweather may have been the epitome of the decline of human morals in the late 1950's. In one of the most notable murder sprees in the modern era, Hollywood has recreated the life of Charles Starkweather many times over.

Charles Starkweather is best known for a murder spree that spanned over the course of just a few months. The circumstances surrounding this reign of terror make it unique to the crime community.

Charles Raymond "Charlie" Starkweather was born on November 24, 1938 in the rural city of Lincoln, Nebraska. As was common in the earlier eras of the 20th century, Starkweather was a part of a large family. He was the third of seven siblings to be born. While he was not especially close to his siblings, he shared a normal relationship with each of them with all factors considered.

Guy Starkweather was Charles' father. Guy fit in with most any southern male at the time. He was a hard-working southern man who took great pride in supporting his family the best that he could. Just after Charles was born, the United States entered into World War II. Due to severe rheumatoid arthritis, Guy was not able to serve his country in the war. While many young children were losing their fathers to the war effort in this era, Charles was lucky enough to have his father at home. Also due to Guy's severe rheumatoid arthritis, he was often unable to complete his work as a carpenter. When Guy was not having a medical flare up of his arthritis, he was well-known in the community as a great wood worker who could complete seemingly any task. However, Guy's condition ultimately led to the Starkweather family living a poor life financially, even by rural standards.

Charles' mother was named Helen Starkweather. Helen was the picture of what a mother should be. She went out of her way to stay active and involved in each of her children's lives. When Guy Starkweather would suffer a flare up and be left unable to work, she would supplement the household income by waitressing. Helen was able to balance this work along with her work at home with taking care of seven children. Helen and Charles shared a good relationship, although he would later admit that he felt "forgotten" as he grew in to his teenage years with so many younger siblings in the house.

Overall, Charles held great memories of his childhood. Unlike most of the killers in the 20th century, he had a strong relationship with his family. Beyond a financially poor situation for most of his childhood, the love and family bond in the home was a great situation for a child to be around.

Charles Starkweather did not share the same happy memories of his education as he did of his family life. He was one of those students who changed drastically from his elementary and middle school years to his high school years. The change was most drastic on his classmates, who could quickly see that Charles was hiding anger from his early years.

A look into the elementary and middle school years of Charles reveals much to behold on some sort of explanation as to why he would carry such a burden. Charles notable had a severe speech impediment. His parents were well aware, even in his toddler years, that his speech was quite different than the rest of his siblings. Financial burdens prevented any sort of speech therapy that could help Charles work through his problem. Throughout his elementary and middle school years, he was bullied nearly every day by his classmates. He would find himself at the center of mean jokes. It was strongly due to this fact that Charles struggled socially at an early age. Many of the other students came after him for being different.

Charles' speech impediment was not the only difference he shared with most of his other classmates. Charles also was born with a condition called genu varum. Genu varum is a birth defect that causes legs to be misshapen in a variety of ways. While individuals with this condition learn to cope and eventually even out as they develop more fully, it was yet another source of bullying that Charles endured. With a speech impediment and a birth defect that affected the look of his legs, Charles Starkweather endured treatment from his classmates that no child should have to endure. Even at a young age, Charles learned quickly that people could be mean.

Even through the bullying in his younger years, Charles Starkweather surprisingly showed no signs of lashing out at his classmates. He more or less took the bullying in stride. While he had very few friends and companions outside of his family, he was an alarmingly quiet child at school.

As Charles entered into his late middle school years, a change became evident in Charles. Charles attended Irving Junior High. It is here that many stories of Charles begin in an attempt to explain a possible motive for his actions. Educationally, Charles struggled tremendously in school. He had a hard time staying focused in many of his core subject classes. Upon beginning his junior high years at Irving, his school problems began to grow. There was one subject, however, that Charles excelled at. Starkweather blossomed in physical education.

Like most other boys his age, Charles was beginning to see his body change. The changes in his body, however, were much more rapid and noticeable than most of his other classmates. Charles was among the tallest and most impressive bodied students in the entire school. The once quiet student who endured more than his fair share of bullies in his elementary years now discovered something. He was bigger than everyone else.

That quiet student who had few friends was not the scared, unassuming boy that many of his teachers and classmates felt that he was. In reality, Charles took note of each student who had bullied him growing up. That is not to say that he had a "list" or anything along those lines. However, he knew that how he was being treated wasn't right. More importantly, he knew that he didn't like it.

Charles Starkweather took gym class as a time to 'get back' at all of those students who had treated him so poorly in his younger years. He would frequently get in fights and make fun of students around him. It took no time at all for Charles' reputation to change. Once considered one of the nicest, most well-behaved students in the school district, he was now considered the "bad child" who didn't fear consequence. Apart from a small circle of friends he gained in junior high and high school, many of the students feared Charles. Most of the students did their best to avoid him at all cost. Bob von Busch, one of his select few friends from his childhood, best sums up the change that everyone noticed in Charles.

"He could be the kindest person you have ever seen. He would actually do anything for you if he found a way to like you. He was a hell of a lot of fun to be around, too. Everything was just one big joke to him. His actions would bring that attitude out in the small group of friends he surrounded himself with. But, he had this other side. A darker side. He could be mean as hell. Just downright cruel. If he saw some poor guy on the street who was bigger than he was, maybe better looking than he was, or better dressed, he would try to take the poor bastard down to his size."

With the change in the personality of Charles Starkweather, it was only a matter of time for more changes to happen. It wouldn't be until Charles turned 17 that the next major change would happen for Charles.

When Charles entered his senior year at 17 years old, his reputation had not changed. While he had a strong circle of friends with whom he had, arguably, too much fun with, he still had the same issues that he previously possessed. He struggled mightily in school, notably lacking any sort of motivation in his studies. Charles didn't do well with authority, either. For this and several other reasons, he would drop out of school just one year short of graduating. He would go on to get his first real job at a Western Union newspaper warehouse. While it didn't pay much money, it offered Charles a chance to get out of the school environment that he hated so much.

In 1956, at just 18 years old, Charles Starkweather would meet the person that would change his life forever. The grounds for their meeting is odd in itself. Charles was introduced to a young, 13-year-old girl named Caril Ann Fugate. Charles was dating Caril's older sister at the time of their introduction. Strangely enough, the two became quite close, often confiding in each other with long talks and intimacy. Shortly after, Charles ended his relationship with Caril's sister. Immediately thereafter, Caril Ann Fugate and Charles Starkweather began their relationship.

Charles' job was located right next to the junior high that Caril attended. He would go be with her each and every day after school. He was considered a terrible employee. His employer described Starkweather just after his murder conviction.

"Sometimes you'd have to tell him the same thing two or three times. Even then, he may not do what he was told because he didn't want to be told. Other times, he struggled understanding basic commands. He was by far the dumbest man we had there."

Caril's and Charles' relationship caused major rifts and consequences and both of their families. It was early in 1957 that Starkweather decided to teach Caril how to drive. He allowed her to drive his 1949 Ford. She quickly crashed the car into another vehicle early one morning. The owner of the Ford, however, was not Charles, but his father Guy. Guy agreed to pay the damages with money that he could hardly spare. This was the breaking point for Guy Starkweather. He banished Charles from the family home and ordered him to never return. With dropping out of school, dating a 13-year-old girl, and crashing the family car, Guy had had enough. Charles, greatly angry at the whole situation, agreed to leave.

Caril's family strongly disapproved of her relationship as well. Obviously, it didn't sit well at all with her parents that she was admittedly dating an 18-year-old boy who had a reputation as a trouble maker. Moreover, at just 13 years old, they felt it was entirely inappropriate for her to be with him in any fashion.

Charles' life was now making another major turn. He was hired on as a garbage collector. He would make minimum wage and struggle to get by for the next several months. But this job had a greater impact than what appears on the surface. During the routes, Charles began to form highly nihilistic views. These views basically meant that whatever circumstance he was currently in was how he was destined to live his life. This was an extremely negative view. He had been in poverty his entire life, and seeing his life turn to working a garbage route for minimum wage helped push him to this gloomy outlook.

Also on these routes, Charles began to plan different robberies. He strongly believed that the best way to change his fortune was to 'take what he wanted'. It was during this time that he would form his famous philosophy on life: "Dead people are all on the same level." He would live the rest of his life by this philosophy. He was not at all shy about this fact either. During his trial, he affirmed this philosophy many times. This officially would mark the beginning of a reign of terror.

The story of Charles Starkweather's murder spree is impossible to tell without understanding the relationship between him and Fugate.

To Charles, Caril was his best friend, his partner in crime. She happily went along with whatever he wanted. She readily broke the rules to be with him. He admired that about her. Charles Starkweather always had something to prove. To most of the investigators surrounding the case, Caril likely gave Charles the confidence and motivation to begin his awful streak. Charles was even able to convince Caril to run away with him. While Caril Ann Fugate denies any knowledge of the murders that Charles would commit beforehand, many believe that Charles convinced Caril to murder her whole family. That fact, however, has never officially been proven.

The circumstance that surrounds Charles' first murder is nothing special all things considered. He didn't have ties to the person he murdered. It wasn't a past childhood acquaintance or even someone that he knew. A late November evening would start one of the most notorious murder sprees in recent history.

In the late hours of November 30, 1957, Charles Starkweather entered a service station in his hometown of Lincoln, Nebraska. Starkweather initially intended to buy a stuffed animal as a gift for Caril. However, he wanted to make the purchase on credit. The clerk that evening, Robert Colvert, refused to complete the sale. Charles became enraged as he stormed out of the store. Charles Starkweather would return to the store three times over the next several hours. He made small purchases. Colvert was disturbed at the awkward behavior of Starkweather.

Finally, Charles Starkweather entered the storm carrying a shotgun. An intense struggle ensued over the gun in which Colvert was injured. Starkweather forced Colvert into his car where he drove him to an extremely remote area on the edge of town. Starkweather forced Colvert out of the car, where he robbed him of $100. After another struggle, Starkweather fired a single shot at point blank range into Robert Colvert's head. With this single shot, Charles Starkweather had committed his first murder.

Charles quickly drove back to Caril Ann Fugate. He confessed to her that he had robbed the service station. However, he foolishly denied actually killing Colvert. He professed to Fugate that someone else had killed Colvert.

During the investigation after the murder spree, Fugate admitted that she didn't believe Starkweather. She knew fully that he had, indeed, murdered Colvert. She claimed that she only went along with the story out of fear of Starkweather. Police, however, never believed that she feared Charlie. Their strong suspicion was that the story and potential for what they were to do was a source of excitement for Caril.

During his murder trial, Starkweather made several eerie sentiments regarding this first murder.

"I had transcended my former self. I reached a new plane of existence in which I was outside the law and could commit any crime without guilt or fear of repercussion."

At this point, Caril and Charles knew that it was only a matter of time before word got around that Charles was, indeed, the killer. This first murder would set off a chain of events that were both devastating and, as the timeline will show, extremely fast.

On January 21, 1958, Starkweather hurried off to the home of Caril Fugate. Caril was not home. Fugate's mother and stepfather, Velda and Marion Bartlett, were at the residence. As was known to Charles, they tried everything that they could to separate Charles and Caril. Caril's parents and Charles Starkweather did not get along. When Charles Starkweather began yelling at them and shouting obscenities, they ordered him to leave the premises and to stay away from Caril. Charles, however, had other plans.

Starkweather returned to his car, and came back to the home with the same shotgun from his first murder. He walked right in the front door and shot both Velda and Marion Bartlett at point blank range. Sadly, they would not be the only two people murdered that afternoon.

Also inside the home was the two-year-old daughter of Velda and Marion Bartlett. Little Billie Jean Bartlett was crying relentlessly at the noise and disturbance in the home. Charles Starkweather proceeded to strangle and stab the innocent Billie Jean. Of all the victims of the murder spree, this is by far the most disturbing.

Caril Ann Fugate would arrive at the home less than one hour later. Upon her arrival, Charles and Caril hid the gruesome bodies of Caril's family behind the house. Great debate has long been had as to the circumstance of this murder. While most everyone believes that Caril and Charles agreed to kill her family as a way for her to be able to flee with him, Caril vehemently denied this fact. She claims that she never intended for her family to be murdered, but that she had no choice but to go along with it after Charles murdered them.

Eerily enough, the couple remained in the house until January 27. With the bodies of her family less than 50 feet away, Caril stayed in the home with Charles. It was only after Caril's grandmother became worried that police were notified that something was happening. This spooked Charles and Caril. It was only then did they decide to hit the road.

Fugate and Starkweather entered into his car and fled the home. They intended to leave Lincoln altogether. Many argue that the murder spree was not planned. Based on Charles behavior and mental state as described after his first murder, most think that he was acting on instinct after the Bartlett murders.

The couple fled on January 27, 1958 to Bennet, Nebraska. They drove to a secluded farmhouse of 70-year-old August Meyer. Meyer was a family friend of the Starkweather family. He was a trusted member of the local community that was known for his blue-collar work ethic and his willingness to help anyone. When Caril and Charles arrived at his home, he never gave a second thought to allowing them to enter his home. Upon entering the home, Charles revealed his shotgun. He quickly fired two powerful blast to the head of August Meyer. For no apparent reason, Charles Starkweather also decided to kill Meyer's dog. The 5th victim of the Starkweather murder spree had just been claimed.

The couple spent no time at all at the Meyer house. They took a few valuables and quickly fled the area. Several miles outside of Bennet, Starkweather managed to get their car stuck in the mud on the side of a rural dirt road. Two local teenagers, Robert Jensen and Carol King, came upon their car and offered their help to free the car. When they exited the vehicle, Starkweather brandished his shotgun and forced them to back to their car at gun point. He made them drive Caril and himself back into Bennet. They arrived to an abandoned storm shelter. After they had exited the vehicle, Robert Jensen was shot in the back of the head with the shotgun. Charles then attempted to rape Carol King. King fought with everything she had and was able to hold him off. Frustrated by this, Starkweather shot King in the chest with the barrel just inches away from her body.

During the investigation after his arrest, Starkweather admitted to shooting Jensen, but claimed that Fugate was the one to actually shoot King. While this has never been proven, many believe there is merit to this claim. It is often concluded that Fugate was frustrated that Starkweather had tried to rape King. Upon coming upon the struggle, it is claimed that she picked up the shotgun and fired the shot that killed Carol King.

The couple's next move was to return to Lincoln. Upon entering town, they drove straight to one of the richest neighborhoods in the area. It was here that they entered the home of wealthy industrialist C. Lauer Ward. Lauer was not home, however his wife and their maid were. When the couple entered the home, they immediately stabbed Lauer's wife Clara as well as the housekeeper. To add further death to the scene, Starkweather snapped the family dog's neck, killing it instantly.

Several hours later, C. Lauer Ward returned home. Upon walking in the back door, Starkweather was waiting for him with his shotgun.

Less than three feet into his home, Ward was shot in the head and killed. Caril and Charles then took all of the valuables in the house that they could find. This included jewelry, silver, gold, and art. They filled Lauer Ward's car up and sped off less than thirty minutes after killing him. The couple then drove straight across the state line out of Nebraska.

With all of the gruesome murder scenes being discovered in this short time period, Nebraska police departments, specifically Lancaster County, were scrambling for answers. Upon the Wards' murder discovery, a community lock down was issued. Each home was searched for possible leads and information. Their big break, however, was soon to come.

Having fled to Wyoming, the couple knew that they needed a new car. Ward's car drew too much attention and was wanted by law enforcement. The last murder of the killing spree was soon to take place. Traveling salesmen Merle Collison was asleep in his Buick on the side of the road. The couple drove by and realized their opportunity. Upon awakening Collison, Starkweather delivered a single shotgun blast to Collison's head. They had secured their new vehicle.

Popular culture focuses on this murder precisely for the actions of Caril Fugate. Caril reportedly performed a *coup-de-grace*. As Starkweather had an issue with his shotgun, Fugate supposedly delivered the fatal wound. While Fugate denies this, many believe this to be true. Charles Starkweather described her as "the most trigger happy person" he knew.

To Starkweather's luck, the salesmen's car that he had stolen had a unique push-pedal emergency brake system. He was completely unfamiliar with how to operate it. The car stalled repeatedly as the couple was making their getaway. A passing motorist stopped to offer assistance to the couple. He was immediately threatened with his life by Starkweather and his shotgun. A brief struggle ensued.

During the struggle, a deputy sheriff passed by the scene. As the sheriff exited his vehicle, Caril Fugate ran to the sheriff exclaiming, "It's Starkweather! He's going to kill me!" Starkweather jumped in the car and sped away. With officers in close pursuit, speeds in the chase exceeded 100 miles per hour. With gun blasts raining down on Starkweather's car, a stray bullet shattered the glass next to him causing lacerations. It was at this time that Charles Starkweather gave himself up.

"He thought he was bleeding to death. That's why he stopped. That's the kind of yellow son of a bitch he is," said Sheriff Earl Heflin.

Starkweather and Fugate were extradited back to Nebraska in late January 1958. Initially, he claimed that Fugate had no participation in the murders. After much questioning, his story changed numerous times. He would eventually agree that she was a willing participant.

Fugate claimed that she was held against her will. She claimed that her families lives were being threatened, and she had no idea that they were already dead. The judge firmly believed that she was an active participant. He felt that she had ample opportunity to escape. Caril Fugate was charged with murder and received a life sentence on November 21, 1958. She served 17 ½ years and was paroled. Caril moved to Michigan and changed her name. She married in 2007 and, despite a serious automobile accident that killed her husband and left her seriously injured, is still alive today. She has done only one major radio interview about the killing spree. She has stayed mute on the subject in her years after prison.

Charles Starkweather was found guilty of murder and given the death penalty. He was executed by way of the electric chair at 12:04 a.m. on June 25, 1959 at Nebraska State Penitentiary.

For just under two months, the crimes committed by Charles Starkweather and Caril Fugate can only be described as disturbing. Such senseless killing at the hands of a strange couple in the early years of their life. Many describe Starkweather as a stray dog. He is imaged this way as the animal that gets a taste of blood that can't seem to let it go. For Charles Starkweather and Caril Fugate, they got a taste of blood and strived to kill all that they could. If not for that sheriff driving by their struggle on the highway, the true numbers of this spree could have been exponentially higher. To anyone familiar with the case, Charles Starkweather got exactly what he deserved.

The Wolf Family Massacre

Carina David

The Wolf family massacre

The tale of the murders of Jacob Wolf, his wife and five children, and their hired help who was also a relative by marriage to the family is chilling, to say the least. The only survivor of this horrible crime was little baby Emma who was eight months old at the time of the murder.

There are many different theories out there today about what actually happened. Many people believe different things due to the complex case that it was. Henry Layer, a resident on a neighboring farm of the Wold family and was accused of the murder and sentenced to prison. Things got a bit complicated when he went on to sign 3 affidavits, the first where he admitted his guilt, and the last two when he was pleading his innocence. This caused a lot of tension at that time, and even now, and caused a lot of questions to come up.

It all started just a little while after the murder, two days to be exact. John Kraft and his wife drove into the yard of the Wolf farm. They hooted, and everything was deathly quiet, except they could hear the faint cry of a baby inside the Wolf family home. They hooted once again, and the baby gave a strong cry.

Nobody came out so Mr. Kraft and his wife went inside to investigate. As they walked into the kitchen, they saw no bodies but traces of blood that led to the cellar trap door. When they looked in, that is when they saw the bodies of Mrs. Wolf, three of her daughters and the body of Jakob Hofer, the hired help.

They later came upon the bodies of Mr. Wolf and his two oldest daughters which were covered in hay in the shed. John Kraft tried to phone someone for help but then he noticed the lines had been cut. They then took baby Emma who was worn out from hunger, crying and cold, back to their home to take care of her there. Reports say that she was very weak at that time. They phoned the police and that's when the investigation began. It was just two weeks after the crime when police took Henry Layer into custody and accused him of the murder of the Wolf family, eight victims in total.

In his first signed affidavit, his confession, he said that he left his home and went to see Mr. Wolf about an issue they had been having with Mr. Wolf's dogs. Apparently, the dog had bitten one of his cows and he wanted Mr. Wolf to come look at the cow to assess the damage done. He said that he walked into the house, into the kitchen where Mr. Wolf, his wife, his five children and their hired hand, Jakob Hofer were sitting.

Apparently, Mr. Wolf had told Layer to go away and that when Layer had refused to leave and tried to reason with him, that Mr. Wolf went to get his double-barrelled shotgun out of the front room. According to Layer, there was a struggle and then two shots were fired in a quick succession of one another. If this was the case, these were the two shots that killed Mrs. Wolf and the hired hand, Jakob Hofer. Mrs. Beata Wolf was thirty-five years of age. She was shot in the back at close range. Jacob was shot through the back of his neck, and the bullet severed his jugular vein.

Layer then managed to get the gun away from Mr. Wolf and went to the front room and then took more shotgun shells from where he saw Wolf take the first two shotgun shells from, and reloaded the gun and started shooting the rest of the family. He said he cannot remember who he shot first but he thinks that he started by shooting Mr. Wolf. He says that Mr. Wolf had started running towards the cowshed when he shot him the first time. There were two shots fired again. One at a long distance which went in his back, and the other so close that it ripped three of his ribs away from his spine.

Layer then claims that he then went into the cowshed and found two of Wolf's daughters, Maria and Edna, who were aged 9 and 7, hiding in the corner and that he shot them where they stood. Maria was shot in the back of the head behind her left ear. Edna was also shot in the back of her head at close range.

Apparently, Layer saw the little girls running from the house to the cow shed which is why he went there to kill them. Investigators confirm this as the window in their parents' room which is where they probably were folding clothes, was open wide enough for them to get through. There was also footprint evidence under the window.

Little Liddia who was about five years old at the time, was shot at the back of her left ear and had a second blow to her head with a hatchet. And the youngest victim, little Martha who was three years old was the only one who did not sustain wounds from a shotgun, instead, she died from a blow with the broad side of the hatchet blade to her head.

He went on to cover the bodies of the girls with hay and then placed Wolf on top of the girls and covered him with his coat and with more Hay. He then opened the trap door that lead from the kitchen to the basement and then he threw the rest of the bodies into the basement and then put down the trap door.

When asked why he did not kill baby Emma, he said it was because she was sleeping at the time of the incident and he did not go into that room. He pulled out the telephone wires and he left the house and closed the doors.

He said he picked up all the empty shells and carried them with him. He broke the gun and threw the broken gun and the shells into the slough. He said that he then went to his house which was approximately two miles away. He said he believed he got home about three hours after he had first gone to the Wolfs' farm.

He then added, at the end, as if it was an afterthought that when he finished shooting in the cowshed, he threw three or four empty shells into the hayloft through an open door. This was signed May 13, 1920, not even three weeks after the massacre.

The funeral

The funeral for the murdered family was held in Turtle Lake. There were over 2 500 people in attendance, even though turtle lake only had a total population of 395. People who had heard about the story came from far and wide. This type of crime was unheard of at that time, and up until this day, it remains one of the most horrendous mysteries and horrible murders of time.

At that time there was nobody in custody for the murder of the Wolf family and Jakob Hofer yet, but many had suspicions as to who the culprit might be. There are some reports that accused Henry of being the murder at the time. They say that Henry Layer opened the caskets and gazed at the faces of the dead family members. But, this was actually the norm back then. Everyone was expecting an open-casket funeral.

There were at least two people who helped prepare the bodies for the funeral as they knew that people would see them, so they wanted to make them look as decent and as respectable as possible. The bodies were so badly mutilated that it even caused one of the women who were helping to clean up the bodies faint. Everyone looked at the mutilated faces of the dead family, including Layer. The women held back shrieks and the men held back their tears. This was not a reason to suspect him at the time, although, after being accused of the murder, people did find it very scary that if he did kill them, he managed to look at all of their bodies after the time. This would have had to be a very sick person.

A separate service was held for Jakob Hofer, who was murdered along with the family. It was held at the farm home of his parents, Bernhardt and Caroline Hofer. He was buried with Jacob and Beata Wolf, as well as their five children at the Turtle Lake Cemetery.

Another theory.

Because of all the questions that came up and the fact that so many people were killed without anyone hearing anything lead to many people making up their own theories.

Rumor at the time was that Mr. Wolf was having sexual relations with one of Layer's daughters. There was never ever evidence about this matter but that would have been the perfect motive.

Layer said that he entered the house to talk to Wolf which was also strange because it is well documented that Wolf had two very good sheepdogs which would have alerted him that there was someone at the farm gate. He would have then gone outside to see who it was. This was the custom in that day. No man would just walk into the home of another.

Reports from neighbors also show that the incident of the dogs biting Layer's cattle was not new and it had been ongoing for six months. Neighbors said that Layer and Wolf were not on talking terms. Wolf would not have let Layer into his house, into the kitchen where his wife and children were sitting if these were indeed the circumstances.

Layer says that he threw everybody into the cellar but as shown from pictures of the scene there was one puddle of blood in the kitchen. Also, the body of Jakob Hofer, the hired helper, was the only one that was on the floor right in front of the ladder, so he was the only one that would have been thrown down.

One of the theories is that the murders were committed during breakfast and not at noon. Also that Mrs. Wolf and her three daughters were not killed in the kitchen, but instead in the cellar where they might have been hiding, or made to go by the attackers.

Investigators found the body of Mrs. Wolf behind the ladder and contrary to the statement by Layer; the investigators had originally believed that Mrs. Wolf was indeed shot in the basement which would have made more sense because of where her body was found.

They then theorize that Hofer was probably coming into the kitchen in the morning, and was shot from behind. They then think that the oldest daughters had tried to run away after hearing the events in the kitchen, which is why they fled from the house and into the cow shed and they hid behind the haystack, which is where they were shot.

What was also suspicious was the fact that in his first statement he said that he threw the broken gun and all the shells in the slough, but afterwards he said that he had thrown more shells through an open door. They all landed in a chicken nest, neatly against each other.

The fact that he had said that in an afterthought was suspicious to some. Also the fact that he was the one that found them and reported them made people wonder that if he was the murderer, would he have not hid them instead of reporting it to the investigators. The fact that the shotgun shells were lying there led people to believe that there were two people involved in the massacre and that someone was waiting there for Bertha and Jacob to come from the fields on hearing the gunshots, and then killing them.

What was also questionable about his first statement was the fact that he said the first two shots that went off by accident were the ones to kill Mrs. Wolf and Jacob, although it is highly unlikely to have two accident shots go off and shoot two people. One was shot in the neck and the other behind the ear. There is no saying what distance they stood at and where they were positioned. It is plausible but unlikely.

According to Layer, the shotgun belonged to Mr. Wolf. The shotgun was found by one of the numerous neighbors that had gone to the farm the day after the murder had been reported. Nobody could verify that the shotgun did indeed belong to Wolf. His friends and relatives also did not recognize the gun.

The oldest daughter and Hofer had gloves on when they were killed, which were still on their hands when their bodies were found. This might show that they were working in the field before they were murdered.

Circumstances of the first confession.

On August 10th, Layer signed another affidavit in which he described the interrogation. He said that a few days after the funeral, four men came to his house and told him to go with them to talk about the killing.

While on their way to Washburn, they stopped and captured another man who Layer thought was an escaped convict from the prison. They put both of them in prison. The convict told Layer that he had a way to escape but Layer refused to go along with any of his plans. They saw each other often and the convict would always ask Layer why he was in prison. His reply was always the same – for no reason.

On May 12th, he went to the Sheriff's office and was questioned. This was no normal interview. Layer claims that he was continuously shown pictures of the murder scene. They carried on the interview until the early hours of the morning.

Layer claims that he was threatened. He was told that there was a mob outside waiting for him as they wanted to take the course of justice upon themselves. Apparently, he was told that the only way that he would ever survive was to confess to the crime and go to jail.

He said that they swore at him and took his chair away and made him stand to the point that he got dizzy. He kept saying he was innocent even through all of this. After that, one of the men in the room hit hum on the side of his head, took him by the hair and pulled him around the room.

Layer claims that this man then sat across the table from him and told him exactly how the murder happened, what he was to say, and then he got up, shook a club in his face and then threatened him by saying that if he did not say that, he would beat him to death.

Layer then gave up. He was crying and then said that he would do as they wished. They then called someone in to write down the confession.

More questions

An affidavit signed by a prison barber at the time confirmed the statements in the second affidavit of Layer.

When Henry Layer arrived at the State Penitentiary in Bismarck, North Dakota, that Myrle Cook had just started acting as a barber there. He said that he shaved Henry Layer and gave him a haircut. He said that when he started working on him, he saw that Layer was badly beaten up and that both sides of his face and the top of his head were swollen and it was obvious that he had been beaten by someone.

He asked Layer what had happened. In reply, Layer told him that he was beaten by the man who had charge of him before he was brought to the institution. He apparently broke down and cried very much and kept on saying that he was innocent.

Dr. C. E. Stackhouse said under oath that he had examined Layer and found him to be in a "normal physical condition". He said that there were two areas of ecchymosis on his face, one over each cheek bone and about the size of a silver dollar but that there was no swelling.

Both these affidavits from these persons show that there must have been some sort of incident. But one describes it as not such a big deal, whereas the other said that Layer had been badly beaten and that there was swelling. Will we ever know the truth?

An affidavit signed by Layer's brother-in-law, William Brokofsky was also in support of Layer's petition for a change of plea. William and Henry's wife, Lydia, went to the State Penitentiary of Bismarck, North Dakota to go see Henry on the first Sunday after he was committed. They asked to see and talk to him but they were refused. They were told that Henry was not in a condition to be seen.

A short while after, they went again to see him. This time they got to see and talk to Henry. This was the first time that William had a chance to talk to him since his confinement and Henry kept on telling him he was innocent. He had also told him under which circumstances he had to admit to the crime.

Lydia Layer also signed an affidavit dated December 20, 1920, which said that she and Henry were married and they were well acquainted with the Wold family. The said that she was at home all day on the 22nd of April, and did the usual work which was hers to do.

She said that she knew of her husband's whereabouts and that Henry was working in the fields that day and that he never left the farm during any part of the day. She said that at noon, at the usual hour, Henry came home and ate and then returned to work which was the usual.

Physical evidence – or the lack thereof

There was no physical evidence that could connect Layer to the murders. The case was wrapped up quickly because people were terrified and others wanted the case to be closed quickly.

More about the accused

Henry Layer, born Heinrich C. Layer was born on the 12 of November 1884 is Eigenfeld, South Russia. HE moved to the country in 1886. Lydia was his second wife. His first wife was Mathilda Miller. They had two children who went by the names of Elizabeth Katherina and Edward. The couple was divorced in March 1911 and the children stayed with their mother.

He went on to marry Lydia Brokofsky Hinzman in January 1912. He was sentenced to life in prison on May 13th, 1920. He and his wife were divorced on December 21, 1922. It is believed that they were divorced so that Layer could free his wife from any legal obligations towards him and that she could move on. Layer then died in hospital on March 21, 1925, after having a blood clot go through his heart after receiving an appendectomy. His wife then remarried only after his death, in November 1925.

Authorities said that Layer was a model prisoner and that he had acted as the head man in the laundry. The obituary stated that he was buried in a local cemetery but up until this day, it is not known exactly where he was buried.

Who was Jakob Hofer?

Jakob was the son of Bernhardt Hofer, who is a brother to Emanuel Whober, who married the sister of Beata Wolf, Christina Bossert. He was only thirteen years old at the time of the incident. He is often referred to as the hired help because Mr. Jakob Wolf had hired him to help him with the spring plantation after a boy who was supposed to help him had to decline. He was in fact family.

What happened to little baby Emma?

The incident happened when baby Emma was just eight months old. She was found just in time because she was so weak already from all the crying, the cold, and going without food or anything to drink. Even though her life was spared, one can just think what kind of an impact that would have had on the rest of her life.

Emma was in attendance at the funeral of her family at that very young age. She lived with her mother's sister and her husband but they passed away in the 1930's. After that, she was put into the guardianship of a couple who lived near her hometown, Turtle Lake. She later went on to study teaching.

Emma carried on to live her entire life in the Turtle Lake area. She was married in 1940 to a gentleman named Clarence Hanson. They had three children. Emma lived a happy life and she died on the 16th of October, 2003 at the advanced age of 84.

More tragedy struck

After her husband had gone to prison and they divorced, 5 of the six Layer children went to an orphanage in Minnesota, and only the youngest that was a year old at that stage had stayed with his mother. One of their children, Berthold Layer was killed at age 6. While at the orphanage the children were playing at one of the farm gates.

According to the Fairmont Sentinel, little Berthold had been told to stay away from the wagon that was coming in with sugar beets on the back. All of a sudden the driver, F.C, Fuller, felt the back of the wagon lift up.

Berthold must have fallen underneath it and it drove over him. His skull had cracked at its' base and his death was said to be instant. His siblings, two brothers, and one sister, who had seen what happened. The youngest who was 4 at the time, Edwin, could not understand it and just cried while he tried to console his siblings, Blanche and his brothers Alvin and Emil.

A twist to the tale

In mid-November 1920, new evidence was found on the Wolf farm. John Hofer and his wife and four children were now renting the land. While playing outside, two of the young children made a thrilling discovery. In some bushes not too far from the house, wrapped in an oil tablecloth, were two homemade cloth masks, a woman's worn dusting cap, and a shotgun shell.

The one mask was large and had holes for the eyes and mouth. Another, smaller mask only had holes for the eyes. The empty shotgun shell was identical to the one found at the scene of the crime. One of the masks and the dusting cap had blood on them.

It is believed that this evidence was planted because hundreds of neighbors came to comb over the farm to look for evidence and investigators are sure they would have found it. But it was planted, or just missed; it is believed that these objects were related to the murder. It is believed that these objects could belong to a man and a woman. Are they the murderers? Or were they involved in the murders?

Conclusion

There are certainly some unanswered questions about this case. Many people were hurt by these events. The Wolf family, the Layer family, the Hofer family, and all the people that knew and loved them. It had quite an impact on all the children at that time, as we can only imagine. The murder tore families apart and it still causes confusion to this day. Will we ever know the answers to these questions? Will justice ever be served? Maybe it already has been, and perhaps, it never will be.

THE JUST DO IT KILLER
SARAH THOMPSON

McCamey, Texas. A town of less than two thousand people, out in the scorching Texas desert, where downtown is a stretch of black road with marginally more buildings on either side. McCamey is the type of town that lies, more or less, entirely forgotten by the rest of the United States, down in the deep heat of Texas. It was in McCamey, in 1940, that Gary Mark Gilmore was born. Gilmore would have, perhaps, gone one to live and die a completely unnoticed life if circumstances had been different. As it stands, Gary Mark Gilmore would gain fame through his life for being the first person sentenced to death in the United States in nearly ten years for the crimes that he committed.

On December 4th, in 1940, Frank and Bessie Gilmore became the parents of their second son, Gary Mark Gilmore. Frank and Bessie were married on a whim, and Frank was said to have other wives and families that he otherwise ignored. Bessie was a Mormon from Provo, Utah, but she had been outcast by her community. Bessie and Frank met and married in California, but the both of them eventually moved to McCamey, Texas, where Gary Mark had been born. Gilmore would have three brothers: Frank Jr., Gaylen and Mikal Gilmore. It was in McCamey that Frank and Bessie were living with their first son Frank Jr., and existing under the false name of "Coffman" in order to escape detection from law enforcement. When he was born, Gary Mark Gilmore had been given the name Faye Robert Coffman - Faye, named after Frank Gilmore Sr.'s mother, Fay.

However, the name Faye Robert didn't stick. His mother, Bessie, decided to change it to Gary Mark Gilmore after they left Texas. Moving wasn't uncommon for the Gilmore family. Gary spent most of his childhood moving from city to city throughout most of the Western United States, along with this three brothers and his parents.

Frank Gilmore supported the family during this time with the sale of fraudulent magazine subscriptions. Gary's relationship with his father was rocky, as was the rest of the family's relationship with Frank Gilmore, Sr. He was described as a man with a quick temper, and who was easily angered. He was also a strict father, and one to dole out corporal punishment when and if he saw fit. Frank often did not need a reason to beat his sons, and would routinely whip them with a razor strop, belt or whip.

Frank Gilmore, Sr. did not only take out his anger and violence on his sons. Though this was less frequent, he would also take to beating Bessie. The relationship between Frank and Bessie was also volatile. Gary grew up in a household in which his parents would often take to screaming at one another, and verbally abusing one another with insults and digs at each other's religions. Bessie would even threatened to kill Frank Sr. some nights. The two parental figures of the household were constantly at one another's throats, and it was the source of a lot of distress and frustration and turmoil within the Gilmore family.

Exposure to violence between his mother and father and the crimes of his father did nothing for Gary's disposition. While his other brothers seemed to escape the thrall of their household unscathed, Gary wasn't so lucky. There's no telling what a calmer household would have done for Gary, and if his rocky home life was the root cause for the crimes he would commit and the path he would soon begin to take in life.

Despite the Gilmore family's nomadic lifestyle for the greater part of Gary's children, they finally settled down in Portland, Oregon in the year 1952. Gary was twelve at the time, and like most twelve year olds, he was starting to stretch his legs and discover some semblance of independence and self-identity. During his adolescence, Gary was incredibly intelligent. He tested an IQ score of 133, and throughout his schooling career he tested and scored well on both aptitude and achievement tests. Gary even showed an incredible ability for artistic talent. He was on the entirely right track to being a successful student and graduating from school.

Unfortunately, Gary did not continue down this path. He was in the ninth grade when he decided to drop out of high school. It was then that Gary became caught up in petty crimes, and took to anti-social behaviors. After he dropped out of high school, Gary ran away from home with a friend. They traveled from Oregon all the way down to Texas. There they stayed for several months before finally returning back to Portland. It was at 14 that he finally managed to succumb to his first arrest. He had started a car theft ring with some friends. Rather than put him in jail, law enforcement released him back to his father and all Gary received from police was a slap on the wrist and a warning to keep in line.

Gary didn't take either the warning or the gift seriously. It wasn't any more than two weeks later when Gary found himself back in court on yet another charge for car theft. At this point, the court sent Gary to the MacLaren Reform School for Boys. The MacLaren Reform School was a correctional facility located in Woodburn, Oregon. The boys residing in MacLaren were anywhere from age 13 to 25, and had committed and range of crimes. In retrospect, due to Gary's immense intelligence and his own willful nature, it might have been the fact that he was sent to MacLaren that had redoubled his affinity for crime, or at least his unwillingness to stop.

Gary was released the next year from MacLaren, but he didn't stay out for long. For the next several years, Gary would be in and out of prison for various crimes. In 1960, at 20 years old, Gary was convicted of another car theft. This time, he was sentenced to time in the Oregon State Correctional Institute. He served a minimal amount of time there, and was even released later in the year. It was around this time in 1961, that Gary's father, Frank Gilmore Sr., was diagnosed with lung cancer. It was terminal. Gary's tumultuous relationship with his father was coming to an end.

In 1962, Gary was once more arrested. This time, the crime was much more severe than stealing a car. He was charged with armed robbery and assault, and was sentenced to Oregon State Penitentiary. It was during this stint in prison that Frank Gilmore Sr. passed away from lung cancer. Gary was in prison at the time and was unable to say goodbye, or even receive the news directly from his family. One of the guards that the Oregon State Penitentiary gave Gary the news about his father's passing.

Gary's relationship with his father had never been good. He grew up in a household where his father and mother were always at odds, with him and his brother's caught in the middle. Frank Gilmore, Sr. was brutal, violent and strict on his sons. He went beyond disciplining them when he raised his belt or whip against Gary and his brothers. Mikal had even once described their father as a "cruel and unreasonable man". And yet, despite all of that - despite the years spent moving around at the whim of his con man father, and despite the years spent at the end of a leather strop and watching his father beat his mother, Gary Gilmore was distraught over the old man's death. When he was given the news of Frank Sr.'s passing, Gary tried to end his life by slitting his wrists.

The suicide attempt was unsuccessful, and Gary Gilmore remained alive. He was eventually released back into suicide. For two years, Gary either stayed out of trouble or managed not to get caught. And yet, in 1964, Gary was once more returned to prison - on the charges of armed robbery and assault, once more. This time, Gary was sentenced to fifteen years in prison for his habitual offenses. A prison psychiatrist finally diagnosed Gary with antisocial personality disorder as well as something called intermittent psychotic decompensation. Psychotic decompensation is a term that describes the rapid deterioration of someone's mental health that they had been, up until then, been otherwise maintaining. This, along with Gary's personality disorder characterized by his disregard and often violation of other people's rights and autonomy, make him a perfect package for crime.

By the time he was 30, Gary Gilmore had spent the greater part of his adult life in and out of prison. The intelligence that had heard him such high marks and a promising future when he was a boy didn't disappear over the years. In fact, Gary used much of his time in prison to write poetry and make artwork. It was these talents that initially won Gary conditional release to a halfway house in Eugene, Oregon. In 1972, he was granted permission to live weekdays at the halfway house under the condition that he stay out of trouble and take art classes at the local community college. However, in line with Gary's usual behavior, he ended up never registering for classes at the community college. Within a month of his initial conditional release, Gary Gilmore couldn't resist the siren call of crime, and was once more arrested and convicted on the charge of armed robbery.

Gary Gilmore's behavior in prison turned from quiet poetry crafting to violence, and he was eventually transferred to a maximum-security federal prison in Marion, Illinois. He was transferred there in 1975. Now 35, it was looking like Gary Gilmore would be spending many more years of is still short life in prison. While he was serving his time in Marion, Gary began writing letters with his cousin, Brenda Nicol. Perhaps it was through Gary's particular intelligence that he manipulated her into believing he deserved a second change, or maybe it was Brenda's own idea. All the same, in 1976, Gary was once more given conditional release into the care of his cousin, Brand. He would live with her in Provo, Utah, under the condition that he stay out of trouble. Brenda would help him look for work and aid in his reform, offering Gary a support system that he had not had previously.

Gary began working at a shoe repair store owned by his uncle, Vern Damico. He also worked, briefly, for an insulation company. This rehabilitation seemed to be on the up and up, and Gary's life was being steered clear of all his previous habits. Unfortunately, Gary wasn't able to keep away from his old ways for long. Soon after his foray into a new life, Gary was back into his old habits of drinking, stealing and fighting. He got into a relationship with a 19 year old woman by the name of Nicole Baker. Nicole was both a window and a divorcee and she had two young children at the time that she and Gary got together. Their relationship was casual at first, but it didn't take long for things between Gary and Nicole to become both intense and strained. Perhaps it was from his own parent's relationship that Gary had learned how to interact with others in a romantic sense - that is, he didn't learn very well at all.

Gary soon began imitate his father. He became controlling with Nicole, and threatening. Their relationship was strained both from Gary's violent behavior, as well as pressure from Nicole's family for her to leave him. Gary was having trouble adjusting to life outside of prison, after spending nearly half of his life, and almost all of his adult life, behind bars. His relationship with Nicole was just a precursor to Gary's inevitable inability to reform himself and stay the straight and narrow path.

It all came to a head on July 19th, 1976. Gary Gilmore stopped at a gas station in Orem, Utah. He had been travelling at the time with April, Nicole Baker's younger sister. During this time, Gary and Nicole were still off-again on-again, in an unstable and volatile relationship. It was around 10:30 in the evening that Gary stopped and told April that he needed to make a phone call. He left April in the car and entered the gas station. It was there that he robbed the gas station attendant, Max Jensen, at gunpoint, continuing his affinity for armed robbery. This time, however, Gary took it another step. After Gary had instructed Jensen to give him the money box, he forced him into the bathroom and had him lay down on the floor. Max Jensen obeyed all of Gary's demands, but his obedience was for naught. According to Gary's confession of the crime, he held his gun against Jensen's head and said,

"This one is for me," before firing the gun once. He then stated, "For Nicole", before firing the gun a second time, shooting Jensen twice and then leaving him, dead and bleeding, on the bathroom floor of the gas station.

Leaving Orem behind, Gary traveled back to Provo with April and spent the night in a motel nearby where he left his truck in a service garage to be repaired. The evening after his armed robbery and murder in Orem, Gary robbed a hotel manager by the name of Ben Bushnell, who lived on the property with his family. Much like the victim before him, Ben Bushnell complied with every one of Gary's demands. An eyewitness, motel guest Peter Arroyo, would later describe Gary ordering Bushnell to lie on the floor. Much like Jensen, Bushnell was shot and killed. When he tried to dispose of his weapon that he used in both robberies and murders, Gary managed to accidentally shoot himself in his right hand. Had he not, he might have managed to get away with both killings and continue on to commit more escalated violence. As it were, his bleeding hand alerted the garage mechanic, Michael Simpson, who had seen Gary trying to hide the gun in the nearby bushes.

Michael Simpson wrote down Gary's license plate number after hearing about a shooting at a nearby motel on a police scanner. He called the police and alerted them of the goings on, of Gary's wounded hand and of his disposing of the gun in the bushes by the mechanic garage. Meanwhile, Gary had called his cousin for support, but she was unsympathetic to his plight. She called the police as well, and Gary was taken into custody after law enforcement found him at the edge of town not long after the incident.

Gary Mark Gilmore isn't the most prolific killer in history, or even of his time. He probably wouldn't even be classified as a serial killer, or even a spree killer. It's Gary's particular circumstances that make him so famous, however. It was the same year that Gary Mark Gilmore was arrested for two counts of murder that the U.S Supreme Court upheld a series of new death penalty statutes in the court decision of Gregg v. Georgia. Before that, death penalty statutes had been deemed "cruel and unusual punishment", and therefore deemed unconstitutional. It wasn't until the 1976 Supreme Court decision that the death penalty was reinstated. Perhaps, if this ruling had not occurred, Gary Mark Gilmore would have rotted away in life in prison as many others had before him during the time where the death penalty was not in effect. Gary Mark Gilmore was charged with both the murders of Jensen and Bushnell, though only Bushnell's murder actually went to trial, due to a lack of evidence and eyewitnesses to Jensen's murder—even though Gary admitted to both.

He was held in custody until October 5th, 1976. It was on that day that Gary Mark Gilmore's trail began in Provo. It lasted only two days. Unhappy with his lawyers' lack of cross-examination and lack of their own witnesses for his defense, Gary persuaded the judge to let him take the stand in his own defense. He claimed dissociation and lack of control, and tried to make a case of insanity. His own attorney's called four separate psychiatrists to shoot down this attempt of claiming insanity, showing that Gary had full control and awareness of what he was doing during the crimes. Not even his antisocial personality disorder was enough for him to actually meet the legal definition of insanity. Despite his intelligence and his skilled manipulation tactics, Gary was not able to present a defense for himself. It seemed that he knew when he was beat.

On October 7, 1976, after two days of trial, the jury returned a guilty verdict. They also agreed on the death penalty, due to circumstances surrounding Gary's crimes. This would be the first execution in the United States in ten years, and the first execution that would happen after the Supreme Court decision to allow the death penalty once more.

Gary's mother, Bessie, attempted to sue to for a stay of execution, despite the fact that Gary himself chose not to pursue habeas corpus.

In a unanimous decision, the U.S Supreme Court refused to even hear Bessie's claim, and her son was slated to be executed. A death penalty sentence in modern times includes lethal injection, as it has been proven to be the most humane way of sentencing a criminal to death, unlike the methods of the past such as hanging or the electric chair. During Utah in 1976, however, the only methods available for executions were hanging, or a firing squad. Gary Mark Gilmore had already accepted his fate as the first man to be executed in the United States in almost ten years. To Gary, a hanging had room for error. He told the court, "I prefer to be shot," and chose the firing squad. Thus, his execution was set for 8 am on November 15th.

Despite having accepted his fate, Gary ended up actually receiving a few stays of execution, though he did not seek them out and explicitly did not want them. It was at the hands of the American Civil Liberties Union (ACLU) and his attorneys that drew out his already chosen execution. When his lawyers tried to call of an appeal on his case, Gary opted instead to fire them. He was ready to face his death, and he saw no reason to draw it out any longer. It was this refusal of appeal that drew the ACLU's attention. The ACLU made efforts, hand in hand with the National Association for the Advancement of Colored People to turn over Gary's execution. However, it wasn't entirely for Gary's benefit. They were using Gary's case to benefit the prisoners who were standing on death row throughout the United States, all of whom were now in danger of facing execution now that the Supreme Court had reinstated the death penalty.

Gary's execution got tied up in legalities. He was ready for it to all be over. In November 1976, while Gary was taking part in a Board of Pardons hearing, Gary said this of all the legal attempts to spare his life: "It's been sanctioned by the courts that I die and I accept that." The dragged out legal battle between the courts and the ACLU put off Gary's execution for months, and in the interim Gary attempted suicide twice. His first attempted occurred on November 16th when his first stay of execution was announced. Nicole Barrett visited Gary in prison, despite her having broken off their relationship. They kissed and held one another during Nicole's visit, and the reason for it became clear. Nicole had snuck in sleeping pills. After she had left, Gary swallowed the overdose of pills—while at the same time, miles away in her own home, Nicole Barrett had done the same, the both of them attempting suicide. Gary had not taken enough sleeping pills for the dosage to be fatal. Nicole took a larger dosage of sleeping pills, which resulted in her slipping into a coma for several days. Gary was not finished with attempting to end his life. With or without Nicole, Gary attempted suicide again one month later to the exact day in December. When that didn't work, he took up a hunger strike.

Finally, Gary was given a date for execution: January 17th, 1977. On the night before his execution, Gary requested that he be allowed to have an all-night gathering that consisted of his friends and family. He was granted the request, and spent his last evening surrounded by the people in his life that could be considered his loved ones. Gary's last meal consisted of potatoes and steak to eat, and milk and coffee to drink. For whatever reason, Gary didn't touch his steak and potatoes. The last thing that he had was the milk and the coffee. The next morning, on January 17th, Gary's last stay of execution was overturned at 7:30 AM, and Gary was finally allowed to go through with his execution as he had wanted so many months previously.

At 8:07 AM, Gary was taken behind the prison to an abandoned cannery. He was placed and secured into a chair with a wall of sandbags behind him for the purpose of absorbing the bullets. In tradition of firing squad, five local police were placed behind a cloth with only a small hole for them to put through the barrel of their rifles, aimed directly at his body from 20 feet away. In Utah tradition, the firing squad consists of four men with live rounds and one man with a blank round. This is done, ostensibly, so that the men comprised of the firing squad will never know which one of them fired the killing shot.

When he was asked for any last words, all Gary Mark Gilmore had to say was this: "Let's do it!" A black hood was placed on his head, and the five gunmen were allowed to fire a single bullet into the body of the first man to undergo execution in the United States in almost ten years. Gary's youngest brother, Mikal Gilmore, was allowed to inspect the clothes worn by his brother after his execution. Allegedly, there were five holes left in the clothes, not four. He noted this in his memoir, 'Shot in the Heart', and mused that Utah wanted to take no chances on leaving his brother alive. Mikal's memoir goes in depth into his relationship with Gary, as well as the strained relationship he had with his family, as well as the aftermath of his own brother's execution at the hands of the state of Utah.

Before his death, Gary had requested that his organs be donated to those in need of transplant. Because of his death by firing squad, it can be presumed that some of his internal organs were useless, now riddled with bullet holes - mainly, his heart, where a piece of black cloth had been pinned as a target for the firing squad. Strangely enough, though, two people were able to receive corneal transplants, courtesy of now famed murderer Gary Mark Gilmore. After his autopsy, Gary's body was cremated. In a grandiose decision by his family, Gary's ashes were then scattered from an airplane over Spanish Fork, Utah.

Gary Mark Gilmore is notorious, perhaps not for his crimes, but for when his crimes occurred. He would have otherwise rotted away in prison, unknown but for the people whose lives he had touched, no matter how horrid and terrible that touch may be. It was by virtue of the place and time that he had committed his crimes that gained Gary Mark Gilmore his fame of being the first man executed in the United States since the death penalty had been reinstated. It is more than just those who were involved in his case and legal battles that remember his name. Gary Mark Gilmore is now known for his own battle for execution. He is remembered in both the minds of those involved, as well as the legal histories of the United States.

The Texarkana Moonlight Murders

IRIS HULSE

Texarkana has always been an unusual place. On the east, you have Texarkana, Arkansas, a small town by any other measurement, yet home to the largest population in Miller County. To the west lies Texarkana, Texas, located in rural Bowie County and lucky enough to have its very own Wal-Mart. Together these twin cities make up what is simply referred to as "Texarkana."

Texarkana is a dusty town, built on a foundation of competing railroads and a Mexican border dispute in the 1800s. The town laid low for the next several years, sending off its sons to fight World War I and then II, and welcoming them back home for better or for worse. But no one in Texarkana was prepared for the national attention that came in the spring of 1946. On February 22nd, 1946, a masked serial killer, dubbed the "Phantom Killer" by the *Texarkana Gazette*'s Calvin Sutton, began terrorizing young couples on the town's secluded country roads.

Today, if you search the Internet for information on Texarkana and its morbid history, you will likely be redirected to pages on *The Town That Dreaded Sundown* and its Arkansan producer, Charles B. Pierce. In 1977, decades after the last murders, this film joined the ranks of *Halloween* and *The Texas Chainsaw Massacre* as one of Hollywood's classic horrors, featuring countless local residents as set extras. While the film's accuracy is something to be questioned, it remains a key piece of the town's identity. Visitors can even catch a screening every Halloween at Spring Lake Park, not far from where one of the infamous murders took place.

Texarkana may have embraced its celebrity status, but eighty years ago the town was paralyzed in fear. Within a single spring, five were dead and three were wounded. All in what had previously been a quiet, friendly community.

A Masked Attacker

Just before midnight, on February 22nd, 1946, Jimmy Hollis and Mary Jeanne Larey were finishing up their date in the backseat of

Hollis' father's car. Hollis, 24, and Larey, 19, had been dating for a while, but his parents expected the car (and the lovebirds) home by midnight. Throwing caution to the wind, they parked on a secluded dirt road, known as a lovers' lane, and proceeded to do what young couples will do.

The pair was soon startled by a flashlight, shining through the driver side window and blinding them to whoever stood outside. Hollis quickly composed himself and opened the door, thinking they were being interrupted by an ill-timed police patrol or a prank from some local kids, but they found themselves face-to-face with a masked man holding a gun.

Hollis continued to confront the intruder, telling him, "Fellow, you've got me mixed up with someone else. You got the wrong man." Hollis later said that the masked man muttered something like, "I don't want to kill you, so do what I say." Hollis attempted to calm the assailant, who forced the young man out of the vehicle and demanded Hollis remove his pants, gun pointed squarely at his face. Larey pleaded with Hollis to do as the man said, thinking he would not become violent if they did as he said. Instead the masked man overpowered Hollis, beating him over the head with the revolver. As Hollis lay limp on the cold ground, the attack continued until the sound of Hollis' skull cracking echoed throughout the clearing.

At this point Larey was hysterical with panic, thinking the loud crack of Hollis' broken skull was the sound of him being shot. She told the man they had no money or valuables, attempting to hand the man Hollis' wallet, but he only screamed, "Liar," at her and demanded her purse. Then the masked man told her to run toward the road. Larey ran as fast as she could, but the strange man pursued, continuing to scream, "Liar," at her as she ran.

The assailant eventually outpaced Larey, and forced her to the ground. Larey reported that the man did not rape her, but that assaulted her violent and used his gun to sexually molest her. Larey was afraid for her life, fighting against the weight of her attacker. She eventually managed to escape his grasp, rising up and telling him, "Go ahead and kill me." She then ran to a nearby house at 805 Blanton Street, where she managed to wake up the sleeping woners and pleaded for help. Shortly after, the Bowie County Sheriff, W.H. "Bill" Presley, arrived at what would be the first known Phantom Killer crime scene.

Hollis and Larey were lucky enough to survive this first attack, though they were left with plenty of physical and emotional scars to show for it. Hollis and Larey described their attacker as a tall man wearing a burlap sack with two slits cut for the eyes, though they could not agree on the man's race. Hollis believed the man was white, with tanned skin from working outdoors, while Larey insisted he was a black man because of his mannerisms and "curses." At this point, the attack was treated as a random attempted robbery, it was unknown the chaos that the Phantom Killer would bring in coming months.

The First Kill

In the early hours of March 24th, a truck driver spotted a young man asleep in an Oldsmobile parked on the side of the road. Concerned about the danger of passing traffic, the truck driver ran up to the window, hoping to wake the man and advise him of a better resting area. To the truck driver's horror, the young man was not asleep; he had been shot twice in the back of the head and sat dead in the driver's seat. In the Oldsmobile's backseat was a teenage girl wrapped in a bloody blanket, her body was completely lifeless. These young lovers were not as lucky as the Phantom Killer's first victims.

Richard Griffin, 29, was a retired Navy SeaBee on a double date with his girlfriend of six weeks, Polly Ann Moore, 17, when they pulled over on the highway to have some time alone. They had just finished up dinner with Griffin's sister and her boyfriend at a local café, and Griffin was in no rush to return his girlfriend to her parents' house. Unfortunately, they would never make it home.

Sometime that previous night, Griffin and Moore had pulled over onto the side of the road. It is believed they were approached similarly to the Phantom Killer's first victims, with a blinding flashlight and pointed gun. There was a heavy rainfall over Texarkana that night, so no one would have been out and about to see the killings take place.

Griffin was likely killed first, with two shots from a .32 Colt revolver to the back of his head. Moore, however, had been dragged from the vehicle and sexually assaulted on the cold, wet ground by their attacker. Blood and marks littered the dirt next to the vehicle. After this horror, Moore was also shot and killed by the Phantom Killer. The assailant pulled a blanket from the car's trunk and wrapped her in it before placing her body in the backseat of the Oldsmobile. Any fingerprints and footprints left behind by the killer that night was washed away by the storm.

Griffin's pockets were found empty and turned inside out, and Moore's purse remained at the scene but was emptied of any cash. With the only apparent motive being robbery, questions still remained as to why the crime was carried out so violently. The *Texarkana Gazette*, at the insistence of the Sheriff Bill Presley, made an announcement on March 27th asking residents to not spread rumors or anything else that they did not see with their own two eyes. Despite offering a cash reward, no solid tips ever made it to the police force.

Murder in the Park

Betty Jo Booker, 15, was a straight-A student who was adored by those around her. She worked with Jerry Atkins playing saxophone for a local band, The Rhythmaires, every Saturday night at the local VFW club. On April 14th, she and Atkins, as well as the rest of their band mates, were playing one of their normal shows. Every other weekend, Atkins gave Booker a ride home alternating with a band mate named Ernie Holcomb. This night was Holcomb's night to drive her home, but Booker told Holcomb not to bother because she had a ride set up with an old classmate who was visiting, Paul Martin. Atkins never knew of this change of plans, and until he received a call the next morning he assumed Booker had left with Holcombe, as usual.

Martin's 1946 Ford Coupe was found at 6:30 the next morning by the Weaver family, who were on their way through Texarkana to Prescott, Arkansas. The keys were found still in the car's ignition. Several miles away, in Spring Lake Park, their bodies would be found. Neither the car nor their bodies were anywhere near their destination that night.

Band and classmates claimed that the two were never close to being a couple, and that Booker felt obligated to go out with Martin because of their connection at school. However, no one knows what they were doing pulled over that night, or why they were in that area of town in the first place. No matter what the true story was that night, Booker and Martin would be the Phantom Killer's third and fourth victims.

Like the previous attack, both victims were shot and killed with a .32 Colt semi-automatic revolver. And like the female targets before her, Booker had been sexually assaulted before her murder. After news of the murder was released, hundreds of Texarkana residents flooded the park, hoping to catch a glimpse of the crime scene or help the investigation.

Martin's body was found almost a mile and a half from the abandoned car. He had been shot four times and the ground surrounding his body was covered in his blood.

Booker's body would not be found until five hours later, over three miles from where the car had been found. Booker was found by the Boyd family and Ted Schoeppey, who had joined the community search party to help find the two teenage victims. Booker had been shot twice, and was found with her hand in her coat pocket.

Both bodies showed signs of a struggle against their attacker, yet their fight was unsuccessful. There was no conclusive evidence as to why their bodies were so far from their car.

Booker's missing saxophone played in the running theory of robbery as a primary motive. The police had alerts al over the area, asking people to keep an eye out for a pawned or for sale saxophone matching the serial number of Booker's, and for several months it was considered one of the best leads the authorities had on finding the killer. Unfortunately for the police, on October 24th, six months after Booker's murder, P. V. Ward and J. F. McNief found the saxophone still in its leather case, just yards from where Booker's body had been found. Ward claimed to know what it was as soon as they stumbled upon it. By the time the case and instrument were turned over to the police, the case had already been labeled closed.

A Red Herring

Public panic over the Phantom Killer was at its all-time high when Virgil and Katie Starks were attacked in their modest farmhouse just ten miles out of town. However, questions would eventually emerge over whether this was truly the work of the Phantom Killer, or if someone else was responsible for the crime.

On the quiet night of May 3^{rd,} Virgil, 36, was reading the Texarkana Gazette when two gunshots burst through the front window of their ranch-style home. These bullets hit Virgil in the head, killing him instantly. Katie was lying in bed, already dressed in her nightgown, when she heard the sound of breaking glass. She headed for the living room, where her husband had been seated, only to find him slumped in his armchair, dead. She cried in fear as she reached for the phone, but the attacker shot through her lower jaw, spraying teeth fragments across the Starks kitchen.

In a state of panic and extreme pain, Katie managed to get back up to her feet. She attempted to grab her husband's gun, but was disoriented from being shot. Despite her injuries, she escaped from the house and ran to her sister's down the street. Finding the house empty, she continued to her neighbors' until she found refuge in the Prater house, where the police were finally called. When A. V. Prater answered the door, Katie simply said, "Virgil's dead," before collapsing on the ground. In the time it took for the police to arrive the killer had fled, taking no valuables or anything else of note with him.

Initially, this attack was labeled as another of the Phantom Killer's. It followed the same time pattern as his previous attacks, used a gun as the primary weapon, and targeted a couple. One of the biggest pieces of evidence connecting this attack to the Phantom Killer was a set of unfamiliar tire tracks that matched those found at the other crime scenes. Because of these similarities, many citizens of Texarkana insist that this murder and attempted assault was the Phantom Killer's final blow to the small town's community.

In November 1948, the local authorities made a different conclusion. Another man was arrested and charged with the home invasion and attack on Virgil and Katie Starks. Law enforcement referenced several reasons as to this not being the work of the Phantom Killer, including the fact that the weapon used was a .22 rifle. This change in weapon, as well as the fact this was a home invasion earlier in the evening, pointed police to consider a different suspect entirely.

The town is still home to many skeptics who believe this attack was the Phantom Killer's doing. The crime scene at the Starks home was filled with physical DNA evidence, but at the time DNA testing was only beginning to emerge in the most developed areas of the nation. A little town like Texarkana was nowhere near equipped to handle a case like this, and the DNA evidence was discarded or improperly stored for later testing. While the official stance is that the Phantom Killer was not involved in this attack, the question still haunts many in the area.

A Town In Panic

As the attacks added up, tension in the town of Texarkana grew. After the first and second attack, police forces from both states increased patrols on the town's secluded back roads. A community that had once been friendly, where front doors were never locked and neighbors were always welcome, now grew eerily quiet after sundown.

Businesses saw a decline in customers, especially those catering to the night crowd. Residents were afraid to leave home, even during the daylight, for fear they may become the next target of the Phantom Killer. However, one industry in town became a hotspot for concerned citizens – the local hardware and ammo shops.

Residents bought up guns and ammo like crazy, hoping to be able to defend themselves from the attacks. Deadbolts and other home security devices became commonplace in all the towns households, and some homeowners were even seen setting up booby traps and other contraptions to catch the killer in his tracks.

Many of the town's local high school and college boys rounded up patrol groups. These men would go out at night with baseball bats and other makeshift weapons, hoping to catch the Phantom Killer on the prowl. None of them were ever successful.

Rumors continued to spread and impair the investigations. There was constant news about someone's son being arrested for the murders, or a suspect being charged, but these rumors rarely ever revealed themselves to be true. Police were forced to perform damage control on the stories spreading around town while also conducting their own investigation into the attacks.

Under the Spotlight

After the final attack, at the Starks farmhouse, authorities and media swarmed into Texarkana like never before. The quiet town was buzzing with news reporters from all across the nation, and reports of the murders were spreading to all areas of the country. Texarkana had never experienced the media's curious eye before.

The famous Texas Rangers stepped into the investigation, headed by the well-known Manuel "Lone Wolf" Gonzaullas. Gonzaullas was the first Ranger captain from Spanish descent, and was known for being a ruthless charmer in his day. He spent a great of his time providing interviews for national newspapers and radio broadcasts about the state of the investigation. He was even found one day taking pictures of the Starks crime scene with a young *Life* magazine reporter; neighbors had reported suspicious lights and sounds from the house when Gonzaullas and the woman were found.

While the local press, headed by the Texarkana Gazette, dubbed the suspected serial killer the "Phantom Killer" or "Phantom Slayer," national media clung to a different name: "The Moonlight Murderer." Because of this title, many believe that the murders were all committed under the full moon, when the nights were in fact at their darkest during the time of the crimes.

A Fruitless Investigation

The entire nation was on the lookout for a masked killer terrorizing young couples, with leads coming in from all areas of the South. In all, the authorities considered over four hundred separate suspects, but no one was ever charged with the attacks of that spring. While most of these suspects never received any public attention, the media caught wind of some of the more notable ones.

A middle-aged man from College Station, a Texas town several miles west of Texarkana, was at one point considered a prime suspect. He had previously been caught sneaking up on parked cars, typically with young couples inside, and brandishing a .22 rifle in order to threaten and rob them. While this man was never convicted of murder, many believed him to be the Phantom Killer based on the similar crime and weapon.

In Fayetteville, a young male graduate student of the University of Arkansas committed suicide. In the wake of his untimely death, a note was found containing a handwritten poem and confession to the murders in Texarkana. His military records showed he had showed "homosexual tendencies" during his time with the U.S. Navy, and at the time these tendencies were believed to be a mental disorder related to sexual crimes like rape or assault. Nothing of value ever came from this lead.

Several local residents accused an IRS agent of the crimes, seemingly because of his antisocial demeanor or because he had gotten on the town's bad side. Another man claimed to have committed the crimes during fits of amnesia. Neither of these claims resulted in an arrest.

In 1999 and 2000, several years after the last murder, an anonymous woman called surviving family members of the Phantom Killer's victims, claiming to be his daughter. She apologized for the actions of his crimes and begged for forgiveness from the families. There is speculation over whether these claims are valid, but many believe them to simply be a cry for attention. After all, the primary suspect of the Phantom Killer murders, Youell Swinney, never had a daughter.

Chasing a Criminal

During his time investigating the Moonlight Murders, Max Tackett, an Arkansas law officer, made a puzzling connection. Before each murder a car had been reported stolen and subsequently abandoned on the side of the rode. This information led police to believe that the Phantom Killer was using stolen vehicles to flee the crime scenes, and then dumping them before disappearing into the night.

The next car reported stolen triggered a police stakeout, with law enforcement hoping to find the killer connected to the vehicle. As police closed in on the stolen vehicle, Peggy Swinney was found to be driving. Police seized the car and took Peggy into custody, where she was questioned on how she came to possess the stolen vehicle.

Peggy revealed that Youell Swinney, a known car thief in Texarkana, had given the car to her, but that wasn't all she had to say. Peggy began telling police how Youell was the Phantom Killer, how he had assaulted and murdered all those couples, and how he had made her promise not to tell anyone. She included details of the crimes that had not been given to the public, information only known by police and the killer himself.

Before the police could move in on Youell Swinney, Peggy's story changed. She claimed that her previous confession was a lie, and that Youell was not the Phantom Killer after all. Eventually law enforcement discovered that Peggy and Youell had recently been married, making her unable to testify against her husband at all. While Youell remained an unofficial suspect, it seemed that the police were unable to touch him. But that changed in 1947, when Youell was arrested for auto theft.

At that time, Youell Swinney already had a long criminal record. He had been previously charged with counterfeiting, burglary, and assault, landing him in the Texas State Penitentiary for many years. After his release, he continued his work as a career criminal, but avoided capture for the time being.

During the investigation, police found evidence that Youell had owned a .32 Colt revolver, the murder weapon used to kill the second and third sets of victims, but that he had recently lost the gun in a failed card game. In hi home was also a shirt with the name "Stark" embroidered on the pocket, but it is unknown whether this shirt was actually connected to the Starks murder in the previous year.

With Youell in custody for auto theft, the police attempted to pin him as Texarkana's Phantom Killer. The man had a history of violence and sexual assault, and the record of stolen cars pointed toward his involvement in the murders. Youell never denied his innocence; he simply stayed quiet and refused to work with the police when questioned. A botched injection of "truth serum" during an interview in Little Rock, Arkansas, would eventually end the authorities' questioning of Youell regarding the Moonlight Murders. He was placed in prison for auto theft.

Youell remained in prison until 1973. Many of his cellmates recounted stories that Youell had told them, ones that included intimate details of the Phantom Killer's murder scenes and heavily suggested that Youell knew more than he let on. In 1994, Youell died a free man, never admitting to the Texarkana murders. To this day, most consider Swinney to be the Phantom Killer, even if he never served time for these crimes.

The Missing Woman

On June 1st, 1948, 21-year-old Virginia Carpenter departed Texarkana by train, on her way to her first semester of studying at the Texas State College for Women. She left Union Station at about 3PM, and headed for Denton, Texas and her new life as an educated woman. On the train ride, she met another student by the name of Marjorie Webster, who she shared a taxi with on the way to their dormitories.

Their taxi driver, Edgar Ray "Jack" Zachary, first dropped off Webster at the Fitzgerald dormitories, and then continued on to Brackenridge Hall, where Carpenter would be staying for the term. Zachary reported seeing Carpenter approach two young men in a yellow convertible outside the dorm, saying that she seemed to recognize them and was excited to see them. The next day, Zachary returned to the dorms to deliver some of Carpenter's luggage that she had forgotten at the station. He placed the trunk at the hall's front entrance and left, but no one ever claimed the luggage. That previous night would be the last time Virginia Carpenter was seen.

On June 4th, Carpenter's boyfriend, Kenny Branham, and her mother reported Virginia missing. After being brushed off by authorities, Mrs. Carpenter and other family members left for Denton late in the evening, hoping to help the police find Virginia.

Within several days, there were airplanes, motorboats, and on-foot search parties scanning the surrounding area for any sign of Virginia. Drivers of yellow convertibles were stopped and questioned, and Zachary was questioned by police and subjected to a polygraph test. Carpenter quickly became one of the most famous missing person cases in Texas, with her picture circulating across the country.

Before long, rumors started spreading back in Texarkana. Virginia Carpenter had personally known three of the Phantom Killer's victims, and some started to believe that she had a target on her back. Perhaps the killer had followed her from Texarkana to Denton, just another passenger on the crowded train. Or perhaps the killer was someone that Carpenter knew, like one of the men seen in the yellow convertible to night she went missing. Either way, many believe that this disappearance was connected to the attacks in 1946.

Countless sightings of Carpenter across Texas - riding in a car, buying groceries, or hitchhiking - continued to flow in, but no solid leads were ever discovered. By 1955, Carpenter was considered dead. She had been missing for seven years, and little hope remained of finding her. Despite this, tips continued to emerge on Carpenter's possible whereabouts.

In 1959, a wooden box was found buried with female remains inside that matched Carpenter's physical description. They were sent to Austin for examination, but the landowners soon confessed to digging them up from an old cemetery.

In 1998, a man called the police claiming to know where Carpenter's body was buried. He led police to the grounds of the Texas State College for Women, the school she was meant to attend, but the search came up empty.

Carpenter's disappearance causes some to doubt Youell Swinney's guilt. If her disappearance was a result of the Phantom Killer, the same man who brutally attacked at least three different couples, then this man could not be Swinney. At the time Carpenter went missing, Swinney was being held in prison for auto theft. Maybe Peggy Swinney had a hand in the disappearance of Carpenter, or her abduction was committed by someone other than the Phantom Killer, but it could not have been Swinney.

Phantoms Around the World

Some believe that the Phantom Killer simply moved his crimes to a new location, but it is likely he just inspired other killers to follow his pattern of attack. As the United States reached the height of violent crime and serial killers, attacks cropped up across the country and even abroad. The Phantom Kiiler's *modus operandi* (or M.O.) would become commonplace among serial killers in the coming decades, including the Zodiac Killer, Il Mostro, and the Son of Sam.

In 1946, a young couple was shot in Fort Lauderdale, Florida. Elaine Eldridge and Lawrence Hogan were parked outside Dania Beach when someone approached the vehicle and shot both victims with a .32 semi-automatic handgun. While the weapon used was not a Colt, it remained very similar to the one used in Texarkana. No fingerprints or footprints were found at the scene. With several similarities to the Texarkana attacks, many believed that the killer had relocated across the country. Texas, Arkansas, and Florida police worked together on the investigation, but no major connections were ever revealed to the public.

Located in San Francisco, the Zodiac Killer operated very similarly to the Phantom Killer during the late 1960s. He stalked young people in their vehicles and shot them with a revolver, and his identity remains unknown. However, unlike the Phantom Killer who personally avoided the media's attention, the Zodiac Killer was hungry for exposure. His main source of fame comes from sending cryptic notes to the Bay Area press, including four ciphers. Only one of these ciphers was ever solved, but it led the police no closer to identifying a suspect. These notes were examined top to bottom, in hopes of finding the true identity of the Zodiac Killer, but no leads were ever found.

Across the Atlantic Ocean, from 1968 to 1985, Florence, Italy was shook by sixteen murders. Dubbed Il Mostro or The Monster of Florence, the killer shot young couples parked alone in their cars with a .22 rifle. While four different suspects were arrested and charged with these murders throughout the years, the investigation has attracted scrutiny and many believe these men were actually innocent.

While the Son of Sam's identity is known today, his killings reflected those of the Phantom Killer and others. Operating in New York City in the mid 1970s, David Berkowitz killed six victims with a .44 Bulldog revolver. His attacks triggered the biggest manhunt in New York City, and for years women kept their hair short and avoided disco clubs for fear of being Berkowitz's next target. Like the Zodiac Killer, Berkowitz loved taunting the police and media with cryptic letters, where he promised to continue killing until he was caught. After his capture in 1977, Berkowitz enjoyed a bit of morbid celebrity for his crimes, which many reported he seemed to enjoy greatly. He remains in prison today, serving six life sentences.

While it is unlikely that the Phantom Killer actually relocated to be the Zodiac Killer or Il Mostro, some true crime experts believe it is possible. While the Phantom Killer was one of the first of his kind, looking back his killings were not exceptionally unique by today's standards.

It is easy to see how the Phantom Killer and his Moonlight Murders have shaped our ideas of killers today. Urban legends of a mad man stalking young couples in love, scratching on car doors and leaving bloody hooks behind, persist around campfires and in dark corners of the Internet. *The Town That Dreaded Sundown* might live among the likes of Freddy Krueger and Michael Myers, but it is a fictionalized retelling of the very real horrors that haunted Texarkana that year.

RAILROAD KILLER

They called him the 'Railroad Killer.'

Angel Resendiz earned the nickname because of his penchant for committing his crimes near railroads, using the rail cars as his own personal get-away system.

Committing murder after murder, he was able to elude both American and Mexican authorities for over a decade.

EARLY LIFE

A birth certificate found by the FBI listed his date of birth as August 1st, 1960. He was born To Virginia de Maturino in the town of Izucar de Matomoros in the state of Puebla, Mexico. His mother has stated adamantly that the correct spelling of his surname is Recendis not Resendiz although the killer would have over fifty different aliases throughout his lifetime.

Angel had spent his childhood years with relatives and not with his immediate family. According to his mother, he was sexually abused by an uncle and other pedophiles in the town of Puebla. He would spend his youth roaming the streets, robbing, stealing and sniffing glue. Relatives would later testify that Resendiz was routinely beaten as a child, one time being "jumped" by several other youths who beat him so bad that he bled through his ears. Resendiz would leave home for months at a time then suddenly return mumbling about a coming religious apocalypse.

Legal trouble came early for Resendiz as he was caught trying to sneak into the Texas border at the age of sixteen. This would become the first of numerous run-ins with border patrol agents until he finally made it into the United States, making his way to St. Louis and finding work with a manufacturing company under an assumed name. He even registered to vote with his false identification.

In September of 1979, at the age of nineteen, Resendiz was arrested for assault and car theft in Miami. He was tried and sentenced to twenty-years in prison but was released after only six years and sent back to Mexico.

But he wouldn't stay there for long.

Through numerous attempts of trial and error, Resendiz had learned not only to game the system but to enter and exit the United States with minimal detection.

He learn to use the rail-cars...

AN "INVISIBLE" MAN

Resendiz became so skilled at crossing the border without detection that he began charging for his services. He began to make a living as a human smuggler, transporting Mexicans across the border for a fee.

Resendiz soon developed a reputation for his smuggling skills, often being seen as a 'go to' person in his Ciudad Juarez neighborhood called 'Patria.'

He would make weekly crossings over the border, being arrested only intermittently. He would then be deported back into his native land only to ping-pong back and forth.

Finally, Resendiz would serve prison terms for his crimes. He would be arrested in Texas for false identity and citizenship, getting a year and half worth of jail.

Upon release in 1987, he journeyed to New Orleans and was arrested for carrying a concealed weapon. He received another year and half worth of prison time until parole.

He then went back to his old haunts in St. Louis where he tried to defraud Social Security and receive illegal payments. He got caught and served a three year sentence.

Resendiz then decided small-time burglaries were his deal. He once again illegally crossed the border, journeyed to New Mexico and was caught burglarizing a home. He was imprisoned for eighteen months and upon release he broke into a Santa Fe rail yard, being captured yet again.

"They should have called Resendiz the boomerang man," forensic psychologist Frank Lizzo said. "He knew how to play the game and seemingly had no fear of the system. The system never punished him severely enough for him to stop his crimes, let alone stop crossing the border."

After his last recorded deportation, the killings began.

THE KILLING FIELDS

"He probably started killing somewhere in his late 20s," Douglas said. "He may have killed people like himself initially – males, transients...(he) became angry at the population at large. What America represents here is this wealthy country where he keeps getting kicked out...(he) just can't make ends meet. Coupled with these feelings, these inadequacies, fueled by the fact that he's known to take alcohol, take drugs, lowers his inhibitions now to go out and kill."

Angel's list of victims began in 1986. Continuing to bounce in and out of the United States, he shot a homeless woman and left her for dead in an abandoned farm house. He had met the acquaintance of the woman at a homeless shelter and they became friends. They would later take a trip on a motorcycle together when he felt that the woman disrespected him.

Resendiz would then take out his gun and blow her head off.

The woman allegedly had a boyfriend whom Resendiz shot and killed as well. He said that he dumped his body in a creek between San Antonio and Uvalde. This killing has never been verified aside from what Resendiz revealed to the police during his interrogation sessions.

Five years later, Resendiz would kill Michael White because he was a "homosexual." Resendiz would bludgeon White to death with a brick and leave him in front of an abandoned home.

These were seemingly warm-ups for the more brutal crimes to come which would also include rape.

"Sex seemed almost secondary," FBI profiler John Douglas said when apprised of Resendiz's crimes. "(He is) just a bungling crook ...very disorganized."

Douglas would later concede, however, that it was this disorganization that worked in his favor. Like a true drifter, Resendiz' whereabouts became as elusive as a rational thought in his head.

"When he hitches a ride on the freight train, he doesn't necessarily know where the train is going," Douglas said. "But when he gets off, having background as a burglar, he's able to scope out the area, do a little surveillance, make sure he breaks into the right house where there won't be anyone to give him a run for his money. He can enter a home complete with cutting glass and reaching in and undoing the locks."

"He'll look through the windows and see who's occupying it. The guy's only 5 foot-7, very small. In fact...the early weapons were primarily blunt-force trauma weapons, weapons of opportunity found at the scenes. He has to case them out, make sure he can put himself in a win-win situation."

Resendiz would also leave his weapon of choice up to chance. Whatever the home would have, a statue a mantle piece, a butcher knife, that would become the instrument of murder.

FLORIDA KILLINGS

On March 23rd, 1997, Jesse Howell would be found bludgeoned to death beside the railroad tracks in Ocala, Florida. He was nineteen years old.

"When we got there," Sheriff Patty Lumpkin said. "We see what appears to be a young male, in his late teens or early twenties. Blood around the head area. You could tell by looking at him that he was dead. The first thing I do is make sure that we've got our forensics people on the way, on the medical examiners on the way, and all the investigators that we have called out or either there or en route."

"When those types of things happen it might have been someone who had fallen off a train," Lt. Jeff Owens said. "Or someone who could have been struck by a train."

The authorities quickly ruled out an accident, however, as they examined the body.

"It didn't appear to be an accident," Lumpkin said. "Because if he had been hit by the train the trauma would have been much more extreme. I've seen some deaths from trains and the initial impact from the train would have done more harm to the body."

The forensic team did determine that Howell's body looked as if he were the victim of blunt force trauma.

"We did see a baseball type of cap," forensic scientist Michael Dunn said. "It appeared to have blood on the inside surface of he bill. In addition, there was a pair of wire rimmed eye glasses and one of the eye pieces was missing, one of the lenses was out. This didn't look good either. As we moved closer, we saw that the victim had been dragged to that spot using just the blue jean material around the cuff (of his pants)."

Near the body, they found a brass and rubber coupling. This device was used to link one train car to another. It could also be used as a clubbing weapon.

"It had what appeared to be blood on it (the coupling)," Dunn recalled.

Howell still had jewelry on his person. He wore a gold cross necklace, a watch and a small amount of cash in his pocket. The police ruled out robbery as a motive.

The police did not identify Howell's body right off the bat. They did find a money wire receipt where some money had been wired from Illinois to Florida. The name on the receipt was of a woman named "Wendy."

Police tracked the money transfer to its point of origin which was all the way in Woodstock, Illinois.

Coincidentally, the authorities there were investigating the disappearance of Wendy Von Huben.

Wendy was missing alongside her boyfriend, the nineteen year old Jesse Howell.

"They advised me that they were investigating a John Doe," Woodstock Detective Kurt Rosenquest recalled. "Unidentified male."

Rosenquest then followed up with the investigating team in Florida, sending them the fingerprints and pictures of Jesse Howell.

The Ocala police would then positively identify Howell.

Jesse had met Wendy only months earlier. They had secretly planned to marry and went on a road trip with another couple.

The other couple, however, grew tired of Jesse and Wendy's constant bickering. They demanded to be let out of the car and left. Jesse and Wendy continued into Ocala, Florida where they ran out of money.

Wendy would call her parents in Illinois who would then transfer her $200 via Western Union. The couple would collect the $200 but would not return home.

"We checked Greyhounds," Rosenquest said. "Nobody matching their description ordered buses or train tickets back to the Woodstock area."

Tears were shed as Rosenquest informed Howell's parents that their teen son had been murdered. The investigative team then turned their attention to the disappearance of Wendy.

They held out hope because there were issues between her and Jesse, thinking that perhaps she simply ran off to be by herself.

Police scoured the surrounding areas and used helicopters in all directions around the railroad tracks.

They would find nothing. There was no DNA left behind on Jesse Howell's body either.

Papers and fliers with Wendy Von Huben's information was distributed all throughout Florida up through Illinois.

Authorities also began interviewing the transient population that lived along the railroad tracks.

Two and a half months later, however, Wendy's parents would receive a phone call.

"The phone rang," Rosenquest recalled. "Wendy's father answered the phone. The girl was crying. She said 'I'm sorry. I love you.'"

She would tell the father she was two hours away from Woodstock at a gas station. The father asked for the phone number on the pay phone she was calling from and she said that there wasn't any before hanging up.

The police were not certain that the phone call came from Wendy so they immediately headed out to the gas station where they believe the call took place.

Police tracked down the surveillance video of the gas station. On the video, a woman that physically resembled Wendy entered the gas station.

The phone records, however, revealed that the call did not come from the gas station where the surveillance video revealed a woman who allegedly was Wendy. It came from another gas station where there were fliers posted of Wendy.

Someone had played a cruel hoax as Wendy's parents had added their home number to the fliers

ONE-LEGGED BOB AND A CHANCE DISCOVERY

A year went by without any sign of Wendy.

There was some ray of hope, however, as the railroad authorities called the Ocala police and informed them that the received information from a member of one of the homeless camps. They had a man in custody named "One Legged Bob" who was traveling with a girl and may be responsible for the murder of her previous boyfriend.

"'One Legged Bob' was your typical homeless person," Owens said. "Kinda scruffy. Hadn't shaved in a few days. He had a prosthetic leg that helped him get around. For someone who you might consider crippled, he was far from crippled."

Owens would spend the next eight hours interviewing the only lead he had, a one legged homeless man.

After the grueling interrogation, Owens realized that he had the wrong suspect.

By sheer chance, however, Patty Lumpkin heard about someone they dubbed the "Railroad Killer" during a class she was taking at the FBI.

"They called him the Railway Killer," Lumpkin recalled. "The Angel of Death. He was killing people. Leaving them near the railroad or he was killing them at homes or locations that were close to the railroad.

The FBI knew the Railway Killer as Angel Resendiz.

"We knew that Angel Resendiz was a person that rode the rails across the country," FBI Agent Mark Young said. "We were worried where he'd wind up next. So we decided to make him a top ten fugitive. Maybe the millions of eyes of the public would tell us something."

The strategy worked.

"He was one of the most vile, evil persons that I had ever dealt with," Young said. "It was like every time you turn around there's another murder."

Owens and Lumpkin hoped to talk to Resendiz to query him about Jesse Howell's murder and Wendy Von Huben's disappearance.

"The attorneys representing him at the time in Texas stopped us," Owens said. "They wanted to protect their client from talking. Any defense attorney who represents a criminal will generally tell the person to stop talking to law enforcement."

Resendiz was placed on death row and Texas had a fast execution rate. The two detectives worried that they would lose their chance to interview Resendiz and connect him to the crimes in Ocala.

Owens and Lumpkin decided to mail Resendiz a letter, respectfully asking him if they could interview him. The letter was written in a formal manner and even addressed him as "Senor."

To their surprise, Resendiz responded back and granted them an interview regarding his involvement in Jesse's killing and Wendy's disappearance.

During their meeting, Resendiz was quick to admit that he had killed Jesse. The detectives deliberately withheld information about the killing, holding back details that only the killer would know. But when Resendiz described using a brake coupling from one of the trains, they knew they had their killer.

But they needed to find out what happened to Wendy.

In a follow-up letter, they promised him immunity from prosecution if he agreed to talk. It was a moot point by then as he was already on death row but the detectives still needed permission from Wendy's family to go through with the interview.

In order to receive some sense of closure, the family agreed to the immunity.

"When we get to the prison," Lumpkin said. "We see him coming down the hallway. He (Resendiz) has a waist belt on. It's an electric shock belt and he's chained to the belt. He's just a mild-mannered person but remember that a psychopath or a sociopath doesn't have any feeling. I mean he had dead eyes. He had no feeling in that body. He didn't care about anything."

Resendiz would reveal that he was heading south for work when the train stopped and he spotted Jesse getting off the train for a smoke.

"Resendiz told us that he killed Jesse with a piece of the train coupling," Lumpkin said. "And Wendy was asleep on the train when this took place. And then when they went down the road further somehow he talked Wendy into getting off the train."

Resendiz then raped and strangled Wendy to death.

Resendiz drew a map of where had left Wendy's body. He described burying her in a shallow grave near a canopy of trees. Resendiz would remember that she had a book in a back pack and an army style jacket that he used to cover her fresh grave.

Police would return to the site and were able to locate where he buried Wendy's body. Almost three years after the murder, everything the killer described was still there. The book. The jacket.

And Wendy's body.

"When Wendy ran away she had a small engagement ring," Owen said. "And she had a Winnie the Pooh wristwatch."

The detective would bring those items back to Wendy's parents.

KENTUCKY RAILROAD MURDER

In August of 1997, Resendiz would make his way from Ocala, Florida to Lexington, Kentucky. It was there he would stalk two young college students.

Holly Dunn was a 20-year old junior at the University of Kentucky and it was there she met Christopher Maier.

"Chris Maier was my very good friend," Dunn recalled. "He was just the nicest, kindest man. We decided that we wanted to be more than friends then we started dating. We dated for about three months."

"Chris and I were attending a party. We decided that the party wasn't very fun so we went to go talk a walk by the railroad tracks. We sat down and talked for awhile and when we got up to leave a man came out from behind an electrical box. He had a weapon that he used on Chris. It was some sort of ice pick or screw driver. Something sharp. I guess our immediate thought was he's going to rob us. That's when we realize he wants money we start thinking 'okay, well, you could have our credit card, you can have our ATM card, you can have our car.' Then he started tying up Chris' hands behind his back. And then he came over to me and he took off my belt and that's when I started thinking he doesn't want to rob us."

After tying up Holly, Resendiz then pulled Chris by the shirt across the railroad tracks and into a ditch.

Holly would follow on her knees, pleading for him to stop whatever he was about to do.

"Lie down," Resendiz said, his voice soft but menacing.

"Everything is going to be okay," Christopher said to Holly as Resendiz dragged him into the ditch.

"Shut up!" Resendiz commanded as he gagged Christopher with a sock.

Resendiz then walked off into the darkness. The frightened couple did not know what the psychopath had planned.

"Then he comes with this rock," Holly recalled. "There was no warning, he drops this rock on Chris' head. I'm just thinking 'what just happened?' I don't even know what just happened."

"You don't have to worry about him anymore," Resendiz said to Holly as he got on top of her.

"I went into survival mode, I'm thinking, I mean he's gonna kill me. I may as well fight. I'm gonna fight. He unties my feet and climbs on top of me. I start to kick and scream and hit him but he held that knife or ice pick (to my throat) and said 'look how easily I could kill you.' I stopped everything and then he raped me."

"I memorized his face," Dunn said. "I stared at him and memorized, he had a tattoo on his arm, I was thinking if you have any scars I'm gonna remember your scars, I'm gonna remember your face, I'm not gonna forget it because if I live through this I will get you."

Resendiz completed the sexual assault of Dunn before smashing her head with a rock.

"He hit me five or six times in my face," Dunn recalled. "I think I put my hand up and then I turned over and then he hit me five or six times in the back of my head. He hit me hard. He was trying to kill me. I think I laid there and he thought I was dead."

Resendiz did think she was did as he threw the rock down and ran away from the crime scene.

Holly would suffer severe facial trauma but miraculously survived the attack.

"I had a broken jaw," Dunn said. "Broken eye socket and cuts on the back of my head that they had to staple shut and then I had cuts on my face."

She woke up in a Kentucky hospital, surrounded by family members.

"Everyone was told not to talk about Chris to me. I just said 'Chris is dead, isn't he?' And my Dad actually is the one I said that to and he was like 'yes, he died.'"

TEXAS TERROR

Resendiz would travel to Texas via train and in October of 1988 he flopped down in Hughes Springs. He would enter the home of 87-year old Leafie Mason, attacking the woman with an iron and killing her.

Two months later, Resendiz would sneak into the home of Dr. Claudia Benton, a thirty-nine year old medical researcher who lived in a suburb of Houston near the railroad tracks.

Again, it was a case of a home being to close to the train tracks. The train would provide the perfect cover for the sneaky Resendiz as he realized that the sound of the rail-car racing by would allow him to break in homes without being heard.

He applied the same technique with Benton, breaking into her home, raping then killing her.

Police would find the doctor face down on the floor. Her bedroom soaked in blood, ransacked for any valuables.

He head had been covered in a plastic bag while her body had been covered in a blanket.

"It appears that she (Claudia Benton) was sleeping," recalled Ken Macha, former police sergeant. "He was able to get in and picked up a bronze statuette from the mantle in the living room. He was relentless in beating her. The skull fractures themselves would have been enough to kill her. She was then stabbed in the back with a very large butcher knife."

"Resendiz was brutal, sadistic," said former West University police chief Gary Brye.

Fingerprints and DNA evidence would link Resendiz to the crime.

The problem was they could catch the man that Texas Ranger Drew Carter referred to as "a walking, breathing form of evil."

EVADING POLICE

Seven months later, Resendiz would continue to avoid capture. He remained in Texas, riding the rail cars until coming into the town of Weimar. He would break into the home of Pastor Norman "Skip" Sirnic and his wife Karen. Resendiz smashed a jack hammer into both of their heads, killing them instantly. He would then rape the body of Karen postmortem.

"He would watch these places," prosecuting attorney Devin Anderson said. "He would watch them, wait for them to go to sleep, get in their house and he would strike them before they would even wake up. I thought we have got to catch this guy."

The DNA found at the scene of the Sirnic murders would match those left on Benton. The FBI then realized they had a highly mobile serial killer on the loose...someone who could kill in one town then appear in another town miles away and kill again.

Resendiz was also smart. He would constantly alter his appearance. He'd shave his head. Then his mustache. He'd be clean shaven one week. Unkempt the next. He would wear glasses one week. No glasses the next.

Authorities could not get an accurate description of him other than the fact that he was small.

Resendiz was also able to take advantage of the lack of a coordinated computer system that gave law enforcement the ability to cross-check fugitives. After the Sirnic murders, Border Patrol had encountered Resendiz near the El Paso border but did not find him on the wanted list.

They then deported him back to Mexico.

Within 48 hours, Resendiz was back across the border to resume his killing spree.

"Our computers told us that he was nothing of lookout material," said C.G. Almengor, a supervisor at the border."We really wish he had been in the system so we could have caught him."

Resendiz would be deported no less than seventeen times over the course of his rampage. At no point did authorities make the connection because of his changing appearance, use of different aliases and the lack of a connected system to document illegals trying to come across the border.

A PREFERENCE FOR TEXAS

Noemi Dominguez was a graduate of Rice University who had just recently quit her job as an elementary school teacher to pursue a master's degree.

She was described as "the sweetest, nicest teacher – a darling who went the extra mile."

Fueled by hate, Resendiz would break into Noemi's home and rape her before killing her with a pick ax. He then stole her car and drove to Schulenberg, Texas where he would kill Josephine Konvicka with the same pick ax.

He would leave the weapon embedded in Konvicka's head as well as leave his fingerprints all over the home. He was more than just sloppy, he was getting cocky. He left a newspaper article that described his crimes as well as a toy train...a reference to his nickname as the "Railroad Killer."

Resendiz was also meticulous in approaching his victims.

"He undid the light in her (Noemi's) car," Anderson said. "So when he opened the door it wouldn't come on. That's who were were dealing with. Someone who really knew how to sneak around. Who really knew how to avoid detection."

"He kept killing people. He would not stop. In his mode of transportation, using the railroads was brilliant because they couldn't be monitored. I mean there's thousands of trains and millions of miles of tracks all over the United States."

"I felt hopeless at the time. Because if you're willing to sleep in a train or you're willing to sleep in a field, you can stay lost for a long, long time and I didn't think we were ever going to catch him."

Later that month, Resendiz had journeyed to Illinois, reaching the town of Gorham. He would break into the home of 80-year old George Morber and his daughter Carolyn Frederick. Resendiz would tie Morber to a chair and shoot him in the back of the head with a shotgun. He then raped Carolyn and smashed the shotgun across her head with such force that the weapon broke in half.

Both Morber and Frederick would die from their injuries.

The FBI placed him on their Top Ten list.

They then recruited his common-law wife, Julietta Reyes, and brought her into Houston for questioning from her hometown of Rodeo, Mexico.

Reyes complied with police requests, turning over over ninety-three pieces of jewelry that her husband had mailed to her from the U.S.

Relatives of Noemi Dominguez claimed thirteen pieces. George Benton was able to identify some pieces of jewelry as belonging to his wife as well.

Police would then locate Resendiz's half-sister, Manuela Karkiewicz, who lived in New Mexico. Initially, she refused to cooperate. She worried that the FBI or the police would kill her brother. But Carter convinced her to talk Resendiz into giving himself up.

The FBI knew that Resendiz had made his way back to Mexico after the murders in Illinois and was hiding in his hometown neighborhood of Patria.

Carter was able to get a rapport with Manuela. He convinced her that Resendiz would receive "personal safety while in jail, regular visiting rights for his family and a psychological evaluation."

"I came away with the impression that they (Resendiz' family) definitely had an understanding of right and wrong ... and knew now that what Maturino Resendiz was accused of doing was heinous and wrong ... ," Carter said. "Manuela, especially, came across as a woman of strong faith. There was a very deep emotional strain and burden placed on her in this investigation. She had to make some very difficult choices that impacted her and her family. And, in the end, her actions alone speak to her character."

Carter spent weeks talking to Manuela who in turn "worked a miracle."

They got the serial killer to surrender.

On July 12th, Manuela would receive a fax from the district attorney's office in Harris County which formalized everything that Texas Ranger Carter had promised.

The word passed from Manuela to another relative who acted as a go-between with Resendiz. The relative than came back later that evening and said that Resendiz would surrender in the morning at 9 a.m.

Texas Ranger Drew Carter would accompany Manuela and a spiritual adviser to meet with Resendiz on a bridge that connected El Paso, Texas to Ciudad Juarez.

"When I saw that face there was a little bit of excitement there because I finally said, 'This is going to happen,'" Carter recalled as he remembered Resendiz appearing on the bridge with his dirty jeans, muddy boots and blank facial expression. "He stuck out his hand, I stuck out my hand, and we shook hands."

Resendiz would then surrender to the Texas Ranger.

DEATH PENALTY

Resendiz' attorneys knew that their only hope would be an insanity defense. The Mexican government also got involved, lobbying authorities to spare Resendiz the death penalty

"Insanity was the logical defense because no one wants to believe that there is someone out there who would do things like that," Anderson said. "That was the thing that worried me the most about the case was that jurors would just throw up their hands and say nobody in their right mind could do what he does."

"The thing about what a life sentence with Resendiz would have been, he would have enjoyed it. I mean he would have had pen pals. He would have given interviews if they let him, I mean he would have loved it. And I knew that. And he didn't deserve to live after what he did just didn't. He caused so much pain, so much heartache and so much terror, that's what the whole focus of the trial had to be."

George Benton, the husband of Claudia, would vehemently criticize the Mexican government who support his appeals and domestic opposition to the death penalty.

"(He)looked like a man and walked like a man. But what lived within that skin was not a human being."

"He was small," Anderson said when she first saw Resendiz in the courtroom. "Maybe five- foot five. His forearms though, were roped with muscles. He was scary. Even though he was small you could feel he was dangerous. He looked like a wild animal who'd been caught."

Resendiz looked "timid" in the courtroom and spoke of himself in religious riddles. He claimed he was Jewish and didn't seem effected when he was informed that the prosecution was aiming for the death penalty.

"I don't believe in death," Resendiz, said. "I know the body is going to go to waste. But me, as a person, I'm eternal. I'm going to be alive forever."

The defense said that Resendiz' crimes were caused by head injuries, drug abuse and a family history of mental illness. He has a delusional perception of the world as he believes that he can cause earthquakes, floods, and explosions and that God told him to kill his victims whom they believed to be evil.

He made a living stealing things from his victims and having his wife sell them in Mexico. "That was his job," Anderson said. "And for recreation it was killing the people who lived in the house."

"He was a very intelligent person who worked the system and knew exactly what kinds of things to say to get that defense to work."

The jury, however, would find Resendiz guilty after one hour and forty-five minutes of deliberation.

He was sentenced to die via lethal injection.

"He made it very clear during my conversation with him that he deserves to die," Owens said.

"I want to ask if it is in your heart to forgive me," Resendiz said in his final words. "You don't have to. I know I allowed the devil to rule my life. I just ask you to forgive me and ask the Lord to forgive me for allowing the devil to deceive me. I thank God for having patience with me. I don't deserve to cause you pain. You did not deserve this. I deserve what I am getting."

Resendiz then prayed in Hebrew and Spanish before drawing his final breath.

House of Horror : The True Story of Rosemary West

Mary Gilmore

Unfortunately, it's not unusual in this day and time to turn on the news and hear a warning about a new serial killer roaming our streets. It's horrifying and hard to comprehend what could possibly make a person commit such heinous crimes. What is wrong with this person that drives him or her to commit such an act? The truth is that people have searched for the answers to that question for a very long time. Unfortunately, it still remains a mystery for the most part.

Rosemary West is one of those baffling cases. We will look deeper into her life and learn how her inner demons progressed to becoming one of Britain's most notorious and sadistic serial killers, taking the lives of at least 10 young women and girls.

Most of the information obtained by the authorities came from her husband and partner in crime, victims who escaped or were permitted to leave, and a great deal from her own children. Rosemary has offered very limited insight into the story, even to this day.

Remarkably, she did not act alone in committing these grisly deeds. This story is immensely complex, which I will attempt to sort out and then tie it all together with the union of Rose Letts West and Fred West in their vicious killing spree. There will be accounts of child abuse, rape, sexual deviance, torture, and murder. Rosemary West's crimes were so horrendous; it may be difficult for some of you to read.

Rosemary West's Early Life

Rosemary's mother came into her room one morning to wake her for school. Rosemary probably knew by the familiar expression on her mother's face that this would be one of those mornings that fills her life with constant dread. As she gets dressed, she begins preparing herself for what she knows is probably about to occur.

As she walks into the kitchen, breakfast is the last thing on her mind. Instead, she braces herself for the punishment she is about to receive. Don't misunderstand, Rosemary hadn't done anything wrong, but her father didn't need a reason.

His kind of punishment wasn't a time-out or a swat on the behind as most children receive. His were the kind that affect a child for a lifetime. Rose has no idea whether she is about to be beaten or if she'll endure other horrors that her father is known to inflict.

That is a likely scenario in the life of Rosemary West. Her father was a paranoid schizophrenic. The mental illness along with other problems, made life for her, her mother, and her siblings a nightmare. The abuse was bad enough, but what made it even more terrifying was not knowing from one minute to the next when or why her father's rage would erupt.

As a result of her home life, Rose made bad grades and became overweight. To make her situation worse, she was teased and bullied at school, giving her no relief from the continuous damage to her self-esteem.

There's a possibility that Rosemary's destiny was sealed much earlier in her life. It's not surprising that Rosemary's mother suffered from severe depression. The illness was so debilitating that she received electroconvulsive therapy several times while Rosemary was still in the womb, one of which occurred just before Rosemary's birth. There were some that thought this therapy was the reason for Rosemary's frequent outbursts of anger as well as her inability to do well in school.

Most of us would be unable to imagine a childhood such as the one led by Rosemary West.

Why do They Kill?

There are no exact traits of a serial killer to help us understand what drives them to kill. Some of them come from a two parent loving home while others have divorced parents. Some had abusive parents and others had loving parents.

Some think it's due to a head or brain injury sometime in their life; however, most people that have had brain injuries do not become killers. The majority of serial killers are men who act alone. Rosemary is not only a woman, she also had a partner in her life of crimes. Female killers and couples represent only a small percentage of serial killings.

The Federal Bureau of Investigation did a symposium, which was comprised of 135 experts who have dealt with serial killers in various ways to determine commonalities of serial killings. They determined that there are no definitive common traits. However, the central nervous system is constantly developing in adolescence, which determines a person's social coping system. That is, they develop the way they interact with their peers such as in negotiation and compromise. If it does not develop adequately, it can result in violent behavior.

It would be safe to say that the events of Rosemary West's childhood could be a factor in the choices she made later in life.

Rosemary's Life Before the Murders

Rosemary Letts was the fifth child born to Bill and Daisy Letts in Devon, England on the 29th of November in 1953. She normally went by the shorter version of her name, Rose. As we've seen, Rose's childhood was unlike most other children's. In pictures of Rose at a younger age she had an ever present smile on her face. You wouldn't guess that she was going through hell within the walls of her home.

The Letts family lived in Northam, a charming seaside town in Devon. Neighbors thought of Bill Letts as a nice man; however, they must have thought it strange that they rarely saw his children. When they did, the children were mainly seen walking around in their garden. One neighbor stated that they really didn't seem to be playing at all. They were just walking around and rarely seen outside the walls of the garden.

What they didn't know was that the children weren't allowed outside the walls and were afraid to play because they were forbidden to get dirty.

Although Rose's father constantly punished the children including Rose, he was not as physically abusive with Rose as with his wife and the other children. It was thought that he didn't physically abuse her as much as the others because he thought there was something not quite right about her.

Some people thought that he didn't hurt Rose as much because he was using her for his sexual pleasures instead. Others speculated that Rose learned at a very young age that she could control her father's anger by using sex.

Rose's mother Daisy, eventually left her father. She moved out of their house taking Rose and the other children with her, freeing them from the abusive environment. Remarkably, after a brief time, Rose moved back in with her father who resumed sexually abusing her.

One day, as Rose waited for a bus, she was approached by a man. Rose described him as a dirty man who had disgusting green teeth. She and the man struck up a conversation and even though his appearance was repulsive by most people's standards, Rose became attracted to him. The man's name was Fred West.

West was raising his daughter and stepdaughter at that time so Rose began babysitting the two girls. In addition, Rose and Fred also became a couple.

Fred's Early Years

Fred West, the son of Walter and Daisy West, was born in Much Marcle, England in 1941. He was the second of their six children. Growing up, he was considered to be a nice boy. They appeared to be a normal family, however, Fred's upbringing was perhaps even worse than Rosemary's. According to Fred, the motto around his house by his father was, "Do whatever you want, just don't get caught."

Fred would later reveal to police that incest was a common occurrence in his household. He said his father regularly had sex with his own daughters. Fred also claimed that his father introduced him to bestiality. In addition, it was thought that his mother Daisy took his virginity when he was 12-years-old.

Not surprising, Fred did not do well in school and dropped out at the age of 15. Two years later, he was involved in a tragic motorcycle accident. He received a broken arm and leg and a fractured skull. The head injury put him in a coma for eight days. Afterward, his family claimed that thereafter, he frequently become enraged without warning. Amazingly, two years later, he received another head injury. In this instance, he fell from a fire escape causing unconsciousness for 24 hours.

Fred's history of child abuse and head injuries would certainly coincide with the conceivable characteristics of a serial killer.

At the age of 20, he was caught and arrested for molesting a 13-year-old girl who subsequently became pregnant. He was convicted, but for unknown reasons he was not sentenced to prison. The reason is possibly because the girl's parents and Fred's parents were friends. Even with his family's propensity for deviant sexual acts, they had recently decided to try their hand at getting religion, therefore, they disowned Fred after this latest incident.

Fred had problems keeping a normal job. He landed a construction job; however, he was caught stealing. In addition, he continued to get caught molesting more young girls. It's amazing how he could still be roaming the streets even back at that point.

Shortly after, when West was around 21, he ran into a former girlfriend named Catherine Costello. She was better known as Rena, which was the name she used while prostituting and the name stuck. In addition, Rena was an accomplished thief. Nevertheless, even with her reputation, she was described by neighbors and other acquaintances as a very nice person and an exceptionally good mother.

Even though she was already pregnant with another man's child at the time, things heated up between her and Fred again and they married about two months later. The baby girl was born in February

1963 and was named Charmaine. Rena had another child by Fred a year later and named her Anna Marie. You will hear the names of these two girls in a shocking context later in the story.

Unbelievably, someone gave Fred West a job driving an ice cream van. This wouldn't seem a proper job for Fred the child molester to say the least. For Fred, it was the perfect job with young girls running after him. It was an ideal way for him to find victims.

While working at this job, a four-year-old boy ran into the street in front of his van and the child was killed. After this incident, even though the death was accidental, Fred feared people in the area would seek retribution for the boy's death. He thought it would be in his best interest to move away.

At the time, a woman named Isa McNeil was caring for the West's children. Additionally, Rena had become friends with a young woman named Anne McFall. They all moved with Fred to *The Lakeside* caravan park in Bishop's Cleeve, Gloucestershire, which is where Fred would later live with Rose.

With Fred's sadistic habits still intact, there were soon problems in this odd household. Fred insistently pushed his warped sexual necessities onto all three women. It became too much for his wife, Rena, and the children's nanny, McNeil, so the two of them moved to Scotland. On the other hand, the other woman, Ann McFall, had warmed up to Fred and stayed behind. Besides, she had already become impregnated by him.

Fearful of Fred, Rena and Isa's planned was to keep their departure secret from him and sneak away. Unfortunately, McFall told Fred, which enraged him. He allowed them to leave, but not with the two children, so the two women fled to Scotland. Rena returned frequently to visit her children.

After that, McFall began to pressure Fred to divorce Rena and marry her. Apparently, this didn't set well with Fred. When she was eight months pregnant with Fred's child, she completely vanished. She was never reported missing, but her body was later discovered in a field minus her fingers and toes, which had been removed and were missing.

Fred was left to care for his daughter and stepdaughter.

The Evil Duo Unites

Around this time is when Fred met Rose at the bus stop. It was at the time when Fred was caring for his step-daughter and biological daughter, so Fred already had at least the one murder of Anne McFall under his belt when he met Rose. Rose then began taking care of the two children.

When they first got together Rose was only 16-years-old and Fred was 12 years older at 28. Her father absolutely disapproved of the relationship. He threatened West that if he didn't leave Rose alone he would call Social Services due to Rose's young age. That was ironic since her father had been having sex with her himself for a long time. Of course, that was most likely the reason he didn't want her to go.

Nevertheless, Rose moved in with Fred and they lived together as a family with Fred's two daughters. After only about two months, they married she moved in with him at *The Lakeside Caravan Park* in Bishop's Cleeve, Gloucestershire, where Fred had lived with Rena and Anne.

Of course Fred, a man of few scruples, soon introduced his young and damaged wife to a sadistic world of pornography and urged her into prostitution. Due to Rose's demoralizing childhood, it didn't take a lot of urging for her to become caught up in his world.

Not one to hold down a regular job, Fred's contribution to the income was mainly by thievery. He wasn't very accomplished at that either and was frequently caught and arrested. It wasn't long before he was sent to prison for 10 months, leaving young Rose in charge of his two daughters.

To make matters worse, she had become pregnant and gave birth to her daughter, Heather, in 1970 while Fred was still in jail. Being young in addition to having mental problems, caring for three children was a tall order for Rose and she didn't handle the situation well, to say the least.

To add to the pressure, seven-year-old Charmaine, began to be unruly and Rose was unable to cope with it. Years later, according to the other child, Anna Marie, it was not unusual for both girls to receive severe beatings; however, no matter how bad the beating, Charmaine refused to cry. This infuriated Rose so it's no surprise that Charmaine didn't seem to be around any longer after that.

This is thought to be when Rose committed her first murder. Rose's tendency to lose her temper most likely caused her to loss control and kill Charmaine. Apparently, Rose hid the girl's body, because it's known that Fred disposed of the body after he returned from prison.

Fred would hold this over Rose in the future. On one of the occasions when Rose's father tried to convince her to leave Fred and come home, Fred made a remark that was something like, "Come on now Rose, you know what we have between us." For someone that didn't know Fred, it would sound like an expression of love. More than likely with Fred, it was his not so subtle way of saying, "You can't leave. I have too much on you." She later told her parents that Fred would do anything, including murder.

Fred's first undertaking after returning from jail was to dismembered and dispose of Charmaine's body. For whatever sick reason, as with Anne McFall, he removed her fingers and toes and then buried her. This became the normal process in Fred's body disposal. It was later speculated that Fred and Rose were possibly involved in Satan worship. It is thought by some that removing the fingers and toes of their sacrifices was typical for Satan worshipers.

The next time Rena Costello came to visit her daughter it naturally created a problem when she discovered her daughter's absence, thanks to Rose. As you can imagine, Rena was not happy about her missing daughter and demanded some answers. Therefore, Rose and Fred must have decided that Rena would have to go as well. So this visit to see her little girl resulted in Rena's demise as well. Minus her fingers and toes, she was buried in a field close to the Caravan Hotel where Rose and Fred still lived.

That meant a total of at least three people had already lost their lives courtesy of Fred and Rose West. One each for Rose and Fred and now Rena by both of them.

A brief time later, Rose gave birth to their second child, Mae. They bought a large two-story house in Gloucester; however, there was not much money coming in. Fred started putting up panels in the rooms to create multiple bedrooms called bedsits. They were tiny rooms, which didn't fit much more than a bed. They began renting out these rooms for extra income; however, the rooms served another purpose as well.

By this time, Rose's fulltime career had become *prostitute*. They also began working other women out of the house. One of the rooms labeled "Rose's Room" was dedicated to Rose for turning tricks. Outside the door was a red light, which was lit when the room was in business. The children knew they were not to disturb when the red light was on. The room also came complete with a peephole, which was Fred's method for watching his wife in action and for making videos.

Both Rose and Fred had come from a family where incest was normal. It was not unnatural to them when Rose's own father occasionally came to their house to have sex with her.

In around October of 1972, Rose and Fred hired Carol Owens as a new nanny for their children. She told her story years later stating that Fred and Rose attempted to bring her into their twisted lifestyle. Not wanting any part of it, she soon left their house.

A few weeks later, as she was walking home, Fred pulled up beside her and offered a ride. The next thing she knew he hit her on the head. When she awoke, her hands were tied and Fred was in the process of taping her mouth.

She was told that if she tried to resist, Fred would call in his friends and let them have their way with her and she would then be killed.

They said they would bury her under the paving stones outside their home along with hundreds of other girls. Terrified, she didn't attempt to resist.

Unbelievably, they allowed her to leave the next day and she proceeded to file charges on them. Fred somehow managed to convince the court that the sex was consensual. In addition, Owens decided that testifying against these two could be an unhealthy choice.

The couple was given a meager fine on a charge of indecent assault and then released. She would be the last victim that the Wests' would allow to leave alive.

Years later, she regretted not testifying. She felt that if she had, it could have saved the lives of numerous women and girls and she was most likely correct.

One day, Fred and Rose arrived home and their neighbor, Elizabeth Agius, was outside. She had become friendly with the couple, so Fred stopped for a chat. Just in conversation, she asked what they had been doing, so Fred proceeded to tell her exactly what they had been up to.

He said they were cruising around looking for young girls. He must have felt he needed to explain why his wife would go along with him on such an outing. He said they figured the girls would see Rose and wouldn't be scared to get in the car. She would later say that she thought he must be joking...he wasn't.

Meanwhile, Fred was busy redecorating the cellar. One of the prostitutes that worked in the house later told authorities that she saw black suits, masks, chains, and whips down there. Fred had created his own torture chamber.

Anna Marie, Fred's remaining child with Rena Costello, was the first to be brutalized in Fred's torture chamber. She was bound, gagged, and violently raped as Rose watched. She was only eight-years-old at the time and this treatment would continue for years.

Eventually, Anna Marie moved out of the house to live with her boyfriend, which quite possibly saved her life. Again, letting her go would prove to be a bad move for the Wests later in court. As one of the survivors, a considerable amount of the horror stories came from her.

After Anna Marie's departure, Fred's attentions naturally turned to his daughters Heather and Mae; however, Heather wanted no part of it and resisted. Understandably, she was unable to keep it to herself and told a friend about the horrors happening at home. This would seal her fate, but Fred later claimed to police that her death was accidental.

The life of Rose and Fred West continued filled with the unimaginable. They would go on to have a total of seven children who were born in a short time span. It is believed that three are by Fred, one is by her own father, and the remaining three are from her clients. It almost seemed that their reason for having children was so Fred and Rose would have someone to torture at the times when no one else was tied up in the cellar. You can certainly say with certainty that Fred and Rose West were definitely not loving parents.

The One's That Didn't Survive the Terror

Over the next few years, the abuse of the West's children continued as did the murders of others. At some point, Fred went to work at a slaughter house. It was thought that this is when his already violent habits became even more gruesome. It could have been a factor in his fascination for dismembering his victims.

It is believed the next victim was Lynda Gough who was a personal acquaintance of the West's. She enjoyed participating in some of their sexual activities by sharing sex partners with Rose. However, for unknown reasons she later vanished. Gough's mother came to the West's house looking her daughter and was told that she moved in order to pursue a job. While she was speaking to the woman, Rose was wearing some of Linda Gough's clothing.

Carol Ann Cooper, only 15-years-old, is thought to be the next victim. She disappeared while walking home from the movies.

Evidence showed she died by strangulation, was dismembered, and buried in the garden.

Lucy Partington was in town visiting her family and a friend over the Christmas holidays. She went to the bus station to take a bus back home and most likely Fred, being one to hang out at bus stations asked her if she wanted a ride. As Fred and Rose planned, it is thought that the only reason she let them even approached her was due to the presence of Rose.

It is thought that they kept Partington in captivity for about a week after she vanished because poor Fred showed up at the hospital about a week later with a large laceration needing stitches. Authorities think he received the cut while cutting up Partington.

Shirley Hubbard went missing when she was returning home from Droitwich. There was definitive evidence of her torture. Her head was completely wrapped with tape with only a short rubber tube in her mouth to breath.

Juanita Marian Mott was a former tenant of the Wests'. Her torture was obvious. She was gagged with a binding made of socks, tights, and a bra, which were all stuffed inside each other. She was also tied up with clothes line rope looped around her thighs, arms, wrists, and ankles. This was done with the rope going back and forth around her horizontally and vertically until she was completely immobilized. She also had a rope with a noose, which most likely suspended her from the rafters in the cellar.

Shirley Anne Robinson was one of the prostitutes that worked out of their house who had sexual relations with both Fred and Rose. She became pregnant by Fred, at the same time Rose was pregnant by one of her clients.

Shirley began to get the idea she would like to replace Rose, which is not advisable in this family. Rose demanded that she had to go. She and her unborn child were dismembered and buried in the back garden. The cellar was full of bodies by this time and the back garden became the new burial grounds.

Therese Siegenthaler was a hitchhiker in route from London to Ireland. Some of the evidence showed that like Partington, she was kept alive for close to a week during which time she was likely tortured and raped.

Allison Chambers was the last known non-related victim. She was killed in 1979.

Their oldest daughter, Heather Ann West, was the last known victim. Fred claims he killed her by accident. His story of the "accident" went something like this. He told police that Heather was being extremely insolent so he had to slap her. She then started laughing at him so he was forced to grab her by the throat to stop her from laughing. He said that unfortunately, he must have grabbed her too tightly because she began to turn blue and stopped breathing. He tried to revive her by putting her in the tub and running cold water on her, but it didn't work.

He then removed her clothes and attempted to put her in a garbage bin, but she didn't fit. Back into the tub she went so he could make her smaller, but he first strangled her with a cord to make sure she was dead. He told police he didn't want to start cutting her up and then have her come alive on him.

He also closed her eyes before he started cutting. He said he couldn't dismember her while she was looking at him. He must have been hearing a strange sound because he told police he found the source of a noise when he cut off her head. He said it was a horrible and unpleasant sound like scrunching. He also said that after cutting her up, she fit quite nicely into the garbage bin.

She was later put in a hole that the West's son, Stephen, had dug with the intention of it becoming a fishpond. Fred put Heather in the hole and built a patio over it. Stephen had unknowingly dug the grave for his own sister's burial.

Police also believed that they killed 15-year-old Mary Bastholm in 1968, though they never found her body. The Wests' son Stephen, later told authorities that he believes Bastholm was one of his father's earlier murders because his father boasted about it.

The Evidence Begins to Surface

Oddly, they violently murdered many of their victims, but then set others free after they had finished using and abusing them. Naturally, some of them went to the police.

The released victims were some extremely lucky women to say the least. Their reports finally got the attention of a Detective Constable named Hazel Savage. Savage was also familiar with Fred West and his arrests for thievery and child molestation through the years since the time he was married to Rena Costello.

Fred videoed an incident in which he raped Anna Marie while Rose held her arms. Anna Marie told friends about her home life who in turn told their parents. This and other information got back to Savage.

This enabled the Detective to obtain a warrant to search the West's property. It was the beginning of the needed evidence to finally remove these damaged and dangerous monsters from the unsuspecting public.

Fred was arrested and charged with rape and sodomy of a minor and Rose for assisting in the rape of a minor. Amazingly, Fred and Rose West were still not suspected of murder. At this time, the younger children were removed from the home.

Due to the evidence found in the home, Detective Savage had the suspicion that there was more going on here and she began digging deeper into this strange family. She had a feeling that there was something suspicious concerning the whereabouts of their daughter Heather and she was determined to find out.

For instance, it was noticed in the videos of the West's and their children that was seized from their home that Heather was never present. Also, in interviews with some of the children, they said something that should not come from the mouths of children.

Apparently, there was a common joke around the West house. Fred told the children that he would buried them under the patio with their sister Heather if they didn't behave.

Unbelievably, the case fell apart when two of the main witnesses decided not to testify. Detective Savage continued questioning the children repeatedly to no avail. Fred and Rose had programmed them and put enough fear in them by then that they would no longer say anything to help the case.

However, the evidence together with case workers reporting the family joke about their sister Heather kept Detective Savage searching. It also appeared that another child, Charmaine, was missing as well. Eventually, Savage put together enough evidence to obtain a warrant to dig on the Wests' property.

Soon after that, Rose answered the door to find the police with warrant in hand. She quickly called Fred to tell him the police were about to dig on their property and they're looking for Heather. It turned out that Fred would be of little help because it took him four hours to get home. He came up with some excuse about passing out due to inhaling paint fumes at work.

Could it have been that Fred was busy disposing of evidence such as fingers and toes or perhaps he had a burial he had not gotten around to completing. That will never be determined.

They began searching the house in addition to excavating the garden in February 24, 1994. The dig was originally intended to search for the body of the daughter Heather, which they soon found. Fred was brought in by the police for questioning the next day. He surprised the police by confessing to the murder of his daughter Heather and he repeatedly told police that Rose knew nothing about it.

Fred and Rose must have been up all that night getting their stories straight. It is thought that Fred assured Rose he would take all the blame and she shouldn't worry. Fred was good to his word, at least in the beginning.

Meanwhile, after the attending pathologist began inspecting the bones of Heather, he brought it to the attention of the police that there was an extra leg bone indicating the presence of at least one other body.

After that discovery, Fred decided he should do some damage control by telling police the location of Alison Chambers and Shirley Robinson's bodies. He hoped this would prevent them from doing any more digging.

It was first thought that Fred did this to avoid being categorized a serial killer, which is someone that kills more than three people. Unbelievably, as it turned out, Fred wanted the police to stop digging because he didn't want his cherished home to be torn apart any further.

Nevertheless, they continued and began to find more human bones. Rose was not arrested until around March 4, 1994. Even then, it was only for sex offenses. Fred had trouble deciding for sure if he wanted to protect Rose after all. He would go on the recant his confession that he killed Heather and then later changed his mind again saying Rose was innocent.

In Britain, prisoners are sometimes assigned an "appropriate adult", which is someone that assists and basically befriends the prisoner. This was normally done for juveniles; however, Janet Leach was assigned to Fred. Leach didn't know she was about to become the confidant of a serial killer.

It turned out that Fred became comfortable enough with Leach that he soon told her the whole gory story. She pointblank asked him if there were more victims. Fred responded that there were six more and went on to draw a sketch of his house and garden complete with the locations of the graves.

Fred knew exactly where they were located; however, he had some trouble remembering all their names. He recalled one that had a scar on her hand; therefore, Scar Hand became her name. Another he called Tulip because he thought she was Dutch, although she was actually Swiss.

Fred was now on a roll and confessed to the murders of his ex-wife Rena Costello and ex-lover, Anne McFall. He told leach that he dumped them nearby his childhood home. He then confessed that he buried his step-daughter Charmaine, Fred's child that Rose killed, close to the hotel where they lived in Gloucester. Strangely, Fred would admit to the murders, but he would not admit to the rapes.

Meanwhile, Rose continued to play the role of an innocent woman, denying any involvement in the murders. She went so far as to act horrified at the actions of her perverted husband. When Fred attempted to contact her, she snubbed him not wanting to have anything to do with such a despicable person.

After making bail, Rose moved into a halfway house with her son Stephen and her daughter Mae. The police were not convinced of her innocence and bugged the house. Nevertheless, Rose stuck to it and never spoke of anything that would involve her in murder. Only charges of sexual offense remained against her.

As can be imagined, the town of Gloucester was flooded with the media. The attention had a tremendous impact on the small town. The West's house became known by the appropriate name "The House of Horrors". The residents were in disbelief that this unimaginable crime spree had gone on in their town for 20 years.

The Trial

As it turned out, Fred took the easy way out. He hanged himself in his jail cell by tying together bed sheets leaving Rose to deal with the whole state of affairs.

She was finally charged with 10 of the murders since Rena Costello and Anne McFall were before she was on the scene. She went to trial in October of 1995.

One after another, witnesses took the stand and told their shocking stories. One of the highest drama moments of the trial came with the testimony of Fred's oldest daughter, Anna Marie. She was on the stand for two days. At one point she looked her stepmother straight in the eye as she told a story of sexual abuse and torture that began when she was a little girl of only eight-years-old.

She recalled the incident when she was so savagely raped by her father while Rose held her arms. During the incident, Rose was telling her how lucky she was to have parents to show her how to please her husband when she gets married. She said she was hurt so badly that she couldn't attend school for several days. She also recalled a day that her father strapped her down and raped her while he was home for a quick lunch break. These were only two of the many horror stories she lived.

The second day of her testimony was delayed for several hours because she took an overdose of pills the previous evening.

Another person that offered a wealth of damaging testimony was Fred's *Appropriate Adult* and confidant, Janet Leach. However, she became so stressed that she suffered a stroke during the trial causing another delay. It wasn't until later after the trial's end that Leach could tell police the entire story that Fred confided in her.

One of the key witnesses was Carol Owens who was one of the girls they brought home under the pretense of being a nanny. She was allowed to leave, but only after she endured their sadistic sexual torture. Needless to say, she had tales to tell.

Another witness who is still referred to as Miss A was lured to the West house and saw two naked girls who were being held prisoner. She watched as they were tortured and raped. She was then raped by Fred and sexually assaulted by Rose. She was one of the lucky ones that left that cellar with her life.

It wasn't hard for the jury to come back with a unanimous verdict of guilty on 10 counts of murder. Rose received life in prison.

The Aftermath

The "House of Horrors" at 25 Cromwell Street in Gloucester where nine bodies were found was demolished in October of 1996; however, there seemed to be a curse that affected many of the people associated with Rose and Fred West.

John West, Fred's brother, hanged himself while awaiting his trial for the rape of his own niece Anna Marie.

Anna Marie continued to suffer from the memories of her distorted childhood. In 1999, she attempted suicide by jumping from a bridge. She was rescued, leaving her to live another day with the memory of the horrors from her past.

Stephen West, the son of Rose and Fred, attempted to commit suicide in 2002 in the same manner as his father and uncle by hanging himself. However, it wasn't meant to be because the rope broke.

The actual number of murders will remain a mystery. During his interrogation by the police, Fred stated that there were two more bodies buried in shallow graves that they would never find.

He also told them there were 20 other bodies spread around in various places. He claimed he would show the police the location of one body each year. One wonders if he knew at that time that he would later take his own life and wouldn't be following through with that promise.

Fred took any other secrets he had in his evil little mind with him to his grave. After that, Rose wasn't interested in discussing the matter any further.

According to an article in the DailyMail, dated February 2014, even though Rose West filed for a couple of appeals after she went to prison, she has now decided she never wants to leave her top security jail cell at Low Newton jail in Durham and why would she, her cell is equipped with TV, radio, CD player, and private bathroom. She has never confessed to committing any murders.

Authorities know the women and girls were tortured, raped, killed, dismembered, and buried; however, they don't know the details of many of those crimes. Rose has been asked by numerous people to give those details, but she refuses.

Conclusion

This is an account of actual facts; however, it hard to believe that it's anything other than a fictional horror story.

Even after hearing about the disturbing childhoods of both Rose and Fred West, it's difficult to understand the extent of their warped minds. Even more disturbing is the fact that two people that are this broken can find one another and carry out their evil deeds together.

This story brings us no closer to the answer of what drives serial killers. Both Rose and Fred were abused as children mainly by their fathers; however, it was young women and girls that were the focus of their punishment.

There have been books and a movie made about them to show us how this horrific story unfolds. However, only in our minds can we come close to conjuring up the evil that occurred within the walls of 25 Cromwell Street. We may never know the full extent of the terrors that transpired.

The fact that Fred West is gone and Rose West will never see the light of day should make us all sleep a little more soundly.

www.ingramcontent.com/pod-product-compliance
Lightning Source LLC
Chambersburg PA
CBHW021155240325
23985CB00008B/218